Lisa De Vries

BIG FRESH
FAITH

Revived by the
Power & Presence of God

If you have questions or comments about this resource, please contact:
Lisa De Vries at
www.lisadevries.ca
email info@lisadevries.ca

Acknowledgements

— ·•◉•· —

To the precious Bible study teachers who were used by God to give life and breath to my faith...

Thank you for your service to the Lord, even though you could not know the specifics of who He was teaching through you. I am so grateful.

And thank You Lord Jesus for who You are, for what You do, and for allowing imperfect people to pass on the wonder of your grace.

Table of Contents

········•◦●◦•········

········•◦●◦•···

About the Author

—··•●**●**●·•··—

Lisa has been married to her husband, Greg, for over 20 years and they have 3 children. She enjoys hanging out with her family, spending time with friends, being active, and all things related to God.

Lisa fell in love with Jesus Christ as a young adult. Since this time, she has oscillated between moments of Spirit-infused over-achievement and flesh-drunk failure. The one constant in her life is that Jesus Christ is faithful to her, even when she is not.

Despair and defeat in her early Christian life taught her she could do no good without God. Since then, He has proved, over and over again, that with Him, the unimaginable is possible. This has planted in her a tenacious desire to live smack in the middle of the abundant life promised by Christ. Lisa desires to give God full credit for His work, and finds great joy in participating with Him as He sets others free.

Lisa is a Certified Canadian Counsellor who holds a Master's degree in Counselling Psychology from Trinity Western University. In 2013, she founded Mercy Seat Ministry, where she works as a clinical counsellor and ministry leader.

With you and for you,

Introduction

Hey friend, it's a privilege to walk with you in this season of your life. I wish time were unlimited and I could sit with you to hear about your faith journey through the ups and downs of this fallen world. I wish I knew the specifics of how you have been impacted by what's going on around you and in you. Please know, if I had my preference, we'd talk for hours—laugh together, cry together and seek God together.

Given you have this book in your hands, I know you have a desire to live by faith. And I know you long for the power and presence of God to fuel your life. As such, I am honored to meet you here, where we can dive in to faith in the midst of your beautiful moments and those marked with heartache, pain, challenge or sin.

Together, let's examine, let's discover, let's grapple with the intricacies of faith. Let's consider how to be persuaded by the truth about God, how to be propelled to trust in Him, and how to be filled with hope and certain expectation He will come through as Lord. Let's do this because with faith, our messy lives can please God, and with faith, our wandering minds can agree with Him, and with faith, our broken hearts can be healed so we can love again. I want to assure you that purpose, hope and joy await in the abundance of faith-filled living.

In Chapter 6 of Francis Chan's book, Crazy Love, he challenged readers to consider what came more naturally to them: reverence for God or intimacy with Him. This was a curious question to me. As a result, I started a journey of discovering the role these two factors play in faith. First, this exploration was personal, but in time, I began to realize that understanding these concepts and how they impact faith were powerful tools for assisting others to recover when life circumstances landed them in a faith crises.

Big Fresh Faith is designed to rejuvenate your trust in God by increasing your reverence for Him and deepening your experience of intimacy with Him. Through this journey you will encounter the power and presence of God, and dive into the abundant life He has planned for you.

I hope, when this study concludes, you will be thrilled about God's intentionality. I pray your interactions with Him are revitalized, your persuasion of truth invigorated, and your trust of His promises, character and actions more solid than ever before.

Please know I have thought of you, friend, while I wrote the words in this book. My heart is for you, for your freedom, and for your faith. I feel joy as I anticipate God's beautiful, mysterious ministry to you as you trust Him more and more. I hope all the best for you as you begin this journey.

Teaching Segments:

- Each week begins with an introductory video lesson.
  - These lessons can be streamed or downloaded free of charge at **www.lisadevries.ca/bigfreshfaith/**
  - These lessons are twenty to twenty-five minutes in length.
  - A listening guide is located within each chapter to assist your listening.
  - If you are studying with a group, I suggest you watch the videos when you meet together.

Homework Lessons:

- Each week contains five days of homework.
  - Each day requires approximately forty minutes to complete.
  - If you are studying with a group, I suggest you discuss the homework when you meet together.
  - Most groups do not have time to discuss every point, so place an asterisk beside the question, scripture reference, or statement that most interests or challenges you. This way, you can highlight this point with your group.
  - If you are part of a group that enjoys lengthy discussion or has difficulty completing the homework in one week, consider spending two weeks working through each chapter. Often, this strategy allows more in-depth learning and fosters greater opportunities for sharing within the group.

Scripture References:

- Scriptures are recorded in many versions of the Bible to augment learning.
  - The version used is indicated by abbreviation following the verse reference. The full version names are listed on the copyright page of this book.
  - Participants are welcome to use any Bible version preferred; however, for fill in the blank questions, the quoted version will allow for the easiest participation.
  - If you do not have a paper copy of the version used, you can read it online at **www.biblegateway.com.**

Word Studies:

- In some lessons, Hebrew and Greek words are examined to strengthen comprehension of the English renderings.
  - The corresponding Strong's number is included, should you desire further exploration.

Lord Jesus, as we study together, please lead us by Your power and for Your glory, amen.

Week 1

FAITH FORGES AHEAD

The Object of Faith

··•●•··

Head on over to www.lisadevries.ca/bigfreshfaith/
➤ **Watch the Video Lessons** ➤ **Watch Lesson 1 and follow along below.**

Hebrews 11:1 NIV:

"Now faith is _____ *in what we hope for and* _____ *about what we do not see."*

•·· Faith is only as solid as:

1. the _____ in which it is placed, and

2. the _____ toward which it is geared.

•·· In order to live by faith that can remain steadfast even under trial, it is essential that:

• The object in which the faith is placed is unequivocally _____ than any opposition to it.

• The outcome toward which the faith is geared must be unequivocally _____ by the object being trusted.

Faith in Jesus

•·· Faith in Jesus means:

• To be so persuaded as to the _____ about God that it results in trusting Him with hope and certain expectation that He will _____ _____, or deliver outcomes, consistent with the God we read about in scripture.

•·· If we misunderstand or reject aspects of what is true about God and His promises, we form false conclusions about Him, and place our trust in Him to come through according to

_____ _____, rather than _____

_____.

•·· The root of the problem, however, is _____ God's faulty character, it is the faulty _____ we make about how life ought to be with Him.

•·· It is essential to faith, we know the _____ about the object of our faith AND the outcomes_____ promises.

Suggestions for Prayer

Knowledge gained about God is all for naught if not to impact our relationship with Him.

• Talk to God about what stirs in you from this lesson.
• Ask for the Holy Spirit to convict you of any areas where your faith is placed in something that stands as an idol between you and God.
• Thank God for His willingness to work with you toward greater faith in Him.

Help My Unbelief

Key Verse

Mark 9:24 NIV: *"Immediately the boy's father exclaimed,
'I do believe; help me overcome my unbelief!'"*

Becoming a Disciple

When Jesus taught about what it meant to be a disciple of His, He didn't mince words or worry about sounding attractive. He said:

*"Whoever wants to be my disciple must deny themselves and take up their cross and follow me. For whoever wants to save their life will lose it, but whoever loses their life for Me will find it."
(Matthew 16:24-25 NIV)*

What are we supposed to do with that? His are big words. If you and I want to become students of His, if we want to learn from Him, if we desire to be trained up to be like Him, then His instructions to us are clear. Jesus' pitch to potential disciples in Matthew 16:24 involves three things.

List the instructions below.

1. _____ yourself.

• This means to reject our human instincts to be comfortable and concerned for ourselves.

2. _____ your cross.

• This means to grab onto our crucifixion or death—death of our ego, death of our selfish desires, death of our self-focus, possibly even literal death.

3. _____ Me.

• This means to go into our world just as Jesus did. He was found among the poor, among the needy, among the children, among the sinners and the hated. He went into public places and private places. He had many trying experiences and we are told to follow Him.

What are the two parts to the promise that follows this command? (vs 25)

1. _____

2. _____

Becoming a disciple of Jesus requires faith. What He asks of those who follow Him is too extreme to participate in without faith in Him. The instructions to deny ourselves, pick up our cross, and live like Jesus did, are different then the requirements to join almost anything else.

I can join *Costco* with a low annual membership fee and get great savings year-round. If I find a better deal at another store there is no conflict to shop there as well. I can join the local recreation center for a low monthly membership fee and come and go as I please. In fact, if I pay the fee, I don't have to show up or exercise and I can still be a member.

But Jesus' words demand extravagance. Salvation is a free gift given to anyone who places faith in Jesus Christ, but discipleship will cost our *self*, everything.

To give up comfort, self-preservation, and ego requires we are entirely convinced it will be worth it. We might try-out being a Jesus follower even if we're not convinced of His Lordship when it means sitting in a pew on Sundays, but to be martyred for our faith in Him, we need to be 100% convinced He is God.

> Are you entirely convinced that faith is worth giving up your comfort, your pursuit of self, and your ego? Are you 100% persuaded?

The uncomfortableness of faith exposes the genuineness of faith. When I am pushed to put my faith in action, I rarely feel comfortable. Mostly I feel…I don't know exactly, just not close to comfortable. I feel excited about the prospect of living by faith before I start doing it. I feel elated to look back on how God has revealed Himself to me when I have stepped out in faith before. But in the moment when I cannot see how things are going to shake down, when I don't feel God near me, or when I experience fear because I know I can't make it on my own…it is anything but comfortable.

This places me in such a mix of believing and unbelieving. I believe in Jesus' call to those who want to follow Him. I believe His teachings. I believe He is Lord. But, I can still struggle with unbelief when it comes to stepping out in faith-filled action.

Belief and Unbelief

In Mark 9, there is a story of a father who sought to rid his son of a spirit that had been harming him since childhood. The father's desperation is clear. He first asked the disciples for help to no avail. When Jesus entered the scene, He expressed frustration toward the unbelief among the people, then asked for the boy to be brought to Him.

Read Mark 9:22-24. What is Jesus' response to the father's plea for help?

_____

Can you relate to the father's reply? (vs. 24)   ☐ Yes   ☐ No

If so, describe a time when you experienced similar conviction over unbelief even while yearning to believe.

_____

_____

_____

_____

I feel like this so often. I read the Bible and believe what is written about Jesus. I believe He is part of the mysterious Holy Trinity—fully divine—yet became a man, died on a cross, was raised to life, ascended to Heaven. I believe it all. Yet in a moment when I encounter my own frailty, I can feel overcome with unbelief. I can downplay how all that truth relates to the hurdle looming in front of me. I can question things I've settled over and over again. I can soar with faith in one moment, then cry out for help with unbelief in the next. I wish this weren't true about me, but it is. I wish I were steadier, but I'm not. I wish my faith never wavered, but it does sometimes.

If you can relate, what is the impact of this mix of belief and unbelief upon your faith?

_____

_____

_____

_____

Let's pray about this.

Lord Jesus, we come with our mix of belief and struggling to believe. Please give us courage to stand under whatever You allow so we may prosper in faith. Teach us to be ever more convinced of the truth about You. Teach us to trust You with hope and certain expectation that You will come through on Your promises, in Your character, and in Your actions.

In Jewish culture, the students of a rabbi (teacher) were called his disciples. To be a disciple meant belonging to the rabbi's school of thought, way of life, and values. This was not merely an act of mental assent, rather a deep sense of adherence that caused the disciple to be similar to the rabbi.

Jesus made no qualms about the depth of sacrifice required to be His disciple. The costliness of His instructions forces us to wrestle with whether or not we believe Him enough to risk being like Him. His "deny yourself, pick up your cross, and follow Me," produce a cauldron of questions, bubbling and swirling amidst our believing and struggling to believe.

Faith is not the result of whimsy or tradition. Faith is not inherited or earned through rule-keeping. Instead, faith is tested, and trained through perseverance in the middle of the challenges of life. To experience big, fresh faith, requires diving into the journey of faith development…and it's not an easy one.

There are many virtues I wish we could just will into being. But we don't become patient by wishing for patience, we don't gain self-control by having no temptation to indulge, and we don't learn to have hope in suffering without coming face to face with pain. Faith is the same. To remain convinced by the truth about God—to stay fixed on His character and actions no matter what—requires we experience some *no matter whats.*

Romans 12:3 suggests God distributes varying measures of faith, but I don't think this means He always doles it out like candy at Hallowe'en. It seems to me, God invites us to participate in vast experiences through which He shapes us, He mills us, and He fashions faith in us. These opportunities are invaluable, they're just not very often easy. God's gift of faith is like the work of a master craftsman using a forge.

To Forge

The verb, *to forge,* has three meanings. Let's look at each to see how it resembles the methods God uses to shape us and grow our faith.

1. To form by heating and hammering; to beat into shape

Ugh...that's not fun to write.

Forging is a tedious process that can turn old crowbars into knightly swords, decrepit drill bits into functional knives, lawn mower blades into beautiful sculptures, and old car parts into decorative light fixtures. To do this, metal is placed in a hot furnace or fire pit until it becomes soft, then hammered repeatedly into a new shape. The blacksmith must heat the metal enough for change yet not so much that it cracks or breaks. He must apply pressure enough to transform but not so much that it is crushed under his blows. He must have vision enough to begin and vigilance to carry through to the end.

In my Christian life, I have sometimes felt like a piece of metal being heated and hammered by a smithy who knows who He wants me to be and how to transform me accordingly. I look at His intentions and I trust Him. I look at the potential He somehow sees in me and I am encouraged. I look at His desire to use me and I want to cheer Him on. But when I look at the fire and the hammer I often want to protest. I want to shout things like, "You don't seem to know what You're doing!" "You don't seem to care how this hurts." I want my faith forged, but it's daunting to stand in, without flinching, while the hammer is raised and the heat is penetrating.

Do you relate?   ☐ **Yes**   ☐ **No**

Let's take a look at how this process is consistent with what scripture teaches about the development of our faith.

Read James 1:2-4 NIV and fill in the blanks below.

"Consider it pure joy, my brothers and sisters, whenever you face trials of many kinds, because you know that the testing of your faith produces perseverance. Let perseverance finish its work so that you may be mature and complete, _____ _____ _____ ."

How are we instructed to feel about the trials we face?

      a. miserable   c. joyful

      b. entitled   d. defeated

Why?

_____

_____

This scripture teaches it is through tests and trials—where the heat is high and pressure is mounting—that we become mature and complete. Under hard conditions we learn the wonderful ability to persevere. This process builds us into people who lack nothing. As hard as it is to endure the trials, the prize is immense in appeal, don't you agree?

Let's look at the second definition of *to forge*.

2. To form or bring into being especially by an expenditure of effort

Consider now the idea of *forging ahead*. This means to press on, to keep going, to stay engaged when things are difficult. This reminds me of how athletes train for the win despite the agony along the way.

Read 1 Corinthians 9:24-26. What is the purpose of running a race? (vs 24)

_____

What characterizes athletic training? (vs 25) _____

What is unique about the prize that comes from our efforts to endure spiritually? (vs 25)

_____

We are after a prize that will last forever. To gain victory requires discipline and hard work. I am not talking about salvation here. Salvation in Jesus Christ is a gift of grace which no one can earn through hard work. In contrast, to forge faith demands intense effort at times. To have faith when we are scared is raw. To act out of faith when we simultaneously encounter unbelief is risky. To follow Jesus when we know He asks us to give up our life for Him is vulnerable.

The only way we will endure in trials and be disciplined to train in faith is if we are completely convinced of who God is and how He will act. When we are, we become willing to go where He tells us to go and do what He tells us to do even if it's risky, vulnerable and hard.

The third definition of *to forge* means something contrary.

3. To imitate falsely; fraudulent duplication

To forge also means to imitate falsely or to fraudulently duplicate. In relation to faith, this type of forging suggests imitating or duplicating what looks and sounds like faith, but is not faith at all. For example, a person can attend church, sing, and take communion (which can be expressions of faith) yet not be persuaded in heart and mind about the truth of God. Likewise, a person can quote scripture, yet refuse to place hope in God's character and actions when in distress.

Faith forgery puts forward a facade of trust in God which is not backed by action. You see, we aren't people of faith because we call ourselves people of faith. We can't be followers of Jesus if our living gives no testimony to His life and teachings. To say we are Christians is to proclaim discipleship to Jesus—that means we are committed to live like what He said and did is true and impactful, and then set out to follow in His footsteps.

It's not enough to have great moments of revelation over the truth about God. If these truths don't spur us to action, then we are not demonstrating faith in Him. Faith looks like something. It's detectable. Faith in action must reflect that we are persuaded about the truth of God, confident in Him, and expectant that He will come through; otherwise, we will disprove our words with our actions (or inaction).

Consider the following list of scriptures and answer the questions below.

James 2:14-20   Luke 6:46-49

Matthew 7:21-23   James 1:22-25

Summarize the common theme that is present in these passages.

_____

_____

_____

_____

The last sentence of James 2:17 in the Message makes a powerful summary statement.

> *"Isn't it obvious that God-talk without God-action is outrageous nonsense?"*

This third definition of to forge speaks exactly to this point. Supposed faith that does not spur us to do anything is not really faith at all, it is fake. This type of dissonance between belief and action disproves our faith.

What is your reaction to James 2:17?

_____

_____

_____

_____

Pray to God about the current state of your faith. Ask for conviction from the Holy Spirit if He sees fraudulence in your faith. Talk to God about what is revealed—whether conviction or lack thereof.

_____

_____

_____

_____

I long to live with big, fresh, ever-growing faith. I'm eager to be proven genuine rather than fraudulent. But, I also struggle with unbelief. Sometimes I want my good intentions or my thoughtful devotion to be all that is asked of me. Sometimes to give up my life for Christ is just plain hard. If you feel similarly, pray with me.

Let's pray about this.

Lord, please forge our faith. Make it real. Do whatever You see best to train us and to teach us to endure, so we can flourish with You. Make this based on who You are and what we can count on from You.

More Precious Than Gold

───── ••●•• ─────

1 Peter 1:7 GWT: *"The purpose of these troubles is to test your faith as fire tests how genuine gold is. Your faith is more precious than gold, and by passing the test, it gives praise, glory, and honor to God."*

Faith More Precious Gold

By the world's standards gold is a precious commodity. Dense, soft, and malleable, the element is bright yellow and remains untarnished when exposed to air or water. Gold is a transition metal that can be forged. A single ounce can be hammered into a sheet that covers a five-square meter area. Intense treatments occur to remove imperfections, and to increase purity.

In the Bible, faith is said to be more precious than this metal, yet similarly tested by fire and pressure. Like gold, the value of our faith is determined by purity. Thus, we are subjected to extreme heat, hammered, reshaped, and exposed to harsh elements to burn off the imperfections and up the immaculacy of our faith.

Benefits of Faith

Let's take a closer look at the context for the key scripture today.

Read 1 Peter 1:3-9 NIV, then fill in the blanks and answer the following questions.

In God's great mercy He has given us _____ (vs 3) into:

- living _____ (vs 3) through Jesus' resurrection

- and an _____ (vs 4) that will never perish, spoil, or fade

What is the benefit of faith while we wait for the last times? (vs 5)

_____

How are we to emotionally respond to these truths? (vs 6)

_____

What is the outcome of belief in Jesus even though we do not see Him now? (vs 8)

_____

What is the promised result of your faith? (vs 9)

_____

Take a moment to reflect on what these truths mean for you personally. I welcome you to pray along with me below to help you get started.

> ### Let's pray about this.
>
> *God, in Your great mercy You have given me new life. I have been born into hope through Your resurrection, and into a new inheritance that awaits me in heaven. I place my faith in You and Your promises for my future and while I wait for that time to come, I trust I am shielded by Your power moment by moment. Even though I do not see You now, I am filled with joy as I stand confident in Your salvation of my soul.*

_____

_____

_____

_____

_____

Though Now

At times, a great chasm seems to exist between the promises that bring rejoicing and the impact of the *though now* in verse 6. **Read 1 Peter 1:6-7 again.** "We rejoice, though now for a little while you may have to suffer grief in all kinds of trials." This *though now* is a big deal!

Belief in the significance of God's resurrection and the surety of our inheritance is magnificent, but if those truths do not impact how we trust God in the struggles of the *though now,* we will falter in faith. What we believe about God must penetrate into how we cope, who we turn to, and where we find strength in the trials until then.

In verse 7, we are told the trials we face in the meantime are put before us as what?

        a. torture

        b. punishment

        c. excuses

        d. tests

        e. pleasure

To face these tests causes strain. It often doesn't seem fair and right. We have these incredible truths—we are made new, that we can trust in God's power, and perfection awaits us in heaven—yet we endure lives that are painful and flat-out tragic at times. This can leave us wondering where God is in the midst of all the difficulty.

Does this contrast ever leave you feeling discouraged, confused, frustrated?

☐ Yes   ☐ No

If so, describe a time in your life when you struggled with the apparent chasm between God's great promises and the grind of your present difficulties.

_____

_____

_____

_____

Faith Proven Genuine

Look at the second half of verse 7.

What is the outcome of our faith being proven genuine?

_____

The story of Job speaks to God's willingness to allow tragedy in our lives so that our faith, proven genuine, can give praise, glory, and honor to God. In Job 1:7-12, we listen in on a conversation that occurred between God and Satan concerning Job. God called Job a blameless and upright man, credited with fearing God and turning away from evil. Satan proposed Job's faithfulness was conditional upon his charmed life, and claimed he would curse God to His face if he encountered trials. So, God granted Satan permission to test his theory.

Why in the world would God do such a thing? Does it make you concerned like it has me? Job is one thing, but the thought of God in dialogue with Satan over the condition of my faith is cause for alarm. If God were to grant that evil wretch permission to bring trials upon me to test the genuineness of my faith I'd be ripped by the seeming contradiction to His love for me. I don't like trials. I don't want to suffer. I prefer a different plan. Faith proven by fire burns me up.

This is a conversation I have had with God many times. To my dismay, He still refuses to take my advice on such divine matters. This leaves me no choice but to grapple with His character and His perspective.

I wonder how many people have been impacted by the story of Job. I think of a friend of mine who has faced cancer four times. I think of another who was raped before she was old enough to speak. I think of a mom who buried several children before she turned thirty. There are endless stories in my mind of people who, like Job, have struggled with a depth of anguish impossible to comprehend, yet have chosen not to curse God.

Sometimes as I cried with them, I lunged at God in anger. To hear their wails of agony, moans of desperation, and guttural pleas for reprieve, planted angst and impatience in my soul. In

Have you ever been stopped in your tracks by the adamant refusal of faith-filled heroes to deny God's goodness and faithfulness?

some seasons, I lamented over torrents of evil with fists cocked and fingers pointed at God, ready to demand the use of His sovereignty for what I think best.

Then, I've been stopped in my tracks by the adamant refusal of these faith-filled heroes to deny God's goodness and faithfulness. I've been humbled by their stretch beyond what they can see to express faith in Him with shocking beauty. To witness genuine faith—fervent trust, recurring confidence, insistent hope and expectation when the evidence of life does not support such a stance—is breathtaking. It is unimaginable, supernatural.

I do not purport these people danced through their troubles always smiling, patient and with a clean house. I testify to messy, gut-wrenched wrestling that exhausts mind, heart, and body; and believers who settled over and over again on faith in the Lord against all earthly odds.

I don't like the grueling nature of forging, but I acknowledge that when faith is proven genuine, this trust and belief accomplishes what God promises. Hurt people are surrounded with a shield of hope and power, broken souls are saved, and immense glory is given to God. Despite my reluctance to embrace faith tried by fire, I know firsthand, the viral impact it has on those who stand near. Faith proven genuine through testing births a wildfire for those who want the real deal.

Have you ever encountered someone whose faith inspires your own? If so, explain what it is that inspires you.

_____

_____

_____

_____

If you had the power to do so, would you walk in their shoes? Why or why not?

_____

_____

_____

_____

When Jesus was on earth, He was sold out to God's plan for salvation. He was intentional to keep His eyes fixed on the will of His Father, and stood against the temptation to consider His own comfort above His mission. His faith was genuine. His confidence and assurance in God trumped anything offered in this world.

Read Matthew 16:21-23.

Jesus saw Peter's words as a _____ _____ to Him. (vs 23)

What was wrong with Peter's perspective? (vs 23)

_____

_____

Peter wanted comfort for Jesus (and himself) more than he wanted Jesus to live out His faith in the Father's will. What Peter presented as protective, Jesus recognized as a temptation toward unbelief and a stumbling block to His faith proven genuine. He called Satan out in the deception and in doing so, steeled Himself against failure.

Have you ever been deterred from acting on your faith by those who prefer easier circumstances for you? If so, what was that experience like for you?

_____

_____

_____

_____

Have you ever deterred someone you care about from acting on their faith because you want comfort for him/her or are afraid of what such genuine faith may cost?

_____

_____

_____

_____

Jump to Matthew 16. What does Jesus promise in verse 27?

_____

_____

No doubt challenge exists in grasping this promise and waiting for its fulfillment, but our faith in Jesus is more precious than gold. It brings glory and honor to God, and reward to us in heaven. It is worth it—for us and for the people we hold most dear.

Talk to God about what you have learned today. What part of the lesson impacted you? Tell Him about what stirred in you—pray, ask, communicate with Him about it.

_____

_____

_____

_____

Endurance, Character, Hope

—··●●●··—

— *Key Verse* —

Romans 5:3-4 NLT: *We can rejoice, too, when we run into problems and trials,
for we know that they help us develop endurance. And endurance develops strength
of character, and character strengthens our confident hope of salvation.*

Poured Out

Athletics possessed my deepest affection as a younger woman. The challenge and intensity of competition thrilled me. It drove me to push limits and anticipate pain as a strange intoxication. My identity was prided on mental and physical toughness. Delusions of grandeur were squashed daily by athletes with superior abilities, but my private condolence was to work harder, train longer, and dig deeper than my counterparts.

In the preseason of my third year playing university basketball, I was consumed with the routines of weight lifting, shooting practice, improving my maximum oxygen uptake, and of course, playing the game. One evening, my team was told to run 10K at the close of a two-hour practice, and I remember the satisfaction that washed over me as I predicted affirmation for my grit.

As the run began, I delighted in the cadence of my feet pounding the road. The circular motion of heel strike to propulsion to recovery swing pleased my biomechanical thirst. The output of my muscles was equipped by the heavy work of my lungs in each breath. I was made for this. I was mentally prepared for this. I would catch my teammates soon enough.

With the final approach in sight, I'd passed all but one person. My coach stood at the end of the course and I longed to impress her, so I reached deep inside and sprinted hard to the end. I felt proud of myself. I anticipated that my coach would be pleased with me, too.

As I crossed the finish line, my coach hollered at me, "Lisa, if you've got that much energy left at the end of all this, you've been slacking the whole time!" I felt dumbfounded. My face burned. She was impossible to please. I thought my sprint would communicate I was a hard worker, not a slacker!

Her poignant words haunted me. I toyed with them, turned them over in my mind and tried to prove their fraudulence. My ego wanted no part of her perspective, but the truth in her utterance clamored for my attention.

I lifted weights earlier in the day. We practiced for two hours. Plus, I ran 10 kilometers. If I'd given everything I had in those workouts, I would not have been able to finish so hard. If I'd pushed the limits like I claimed in the annals of my inner dialogue, I wouldn't have been resourced to give so much at the end.

I wanted to see my sprint as evidence of great endurance, but my coach concluded I held back all along. I compared myself to the rest of my teammates and perceived I was superior, but to my coach, the exhaustion that characterized their performances was evidence of unrestrained effort. I deceived myself in exchange for a stroke of my ego. I built a reserve to be tapped only when praise awaited.

I don't want to be a Christian who makes this same mistake. I don't want to meet God face to face only to have Him call my bluff. I don't want to keep a stash of spiritual *umpf* so I can look good if God calls on me. I don't want to make a fantasy out of who I am or what I'm doing so I feel better about my inadequacies.

I want my faith in Christ to be genuine. I want to give all I've got to Him with no regard for what comes next. I want to pour out with abandon because I'm convinced He will deposit new rations as needed. I want to run hard from the starting line. I want to engage with Him moment by moment, so I take hold of what is, not what I pretend.

God will not be wowed by a token sprint here or there. He urges us to give it all. He asks us to trust Him and His provision so fully, that by faith, we give every bit of ourselves—heart, mind, soul, and strength—all the way through this life He planned for us.

Read the key scripture verses for today. What are the three qualities that can develop in us through problems and trials?

1. _____

2. _____

3. _____

According to verse 3, what can our response be to these problems and trials in light of the work they are accomplishing in us?

_____

Endurance

Endurance: HUPOMONĒ (G5281)

The word translated, *endurance* or *perseverance,* in Romans 5:3-4, is the Greek word HUPOMONĒ. This word means:

- to remain under with constancy despite the circumstances
- it implies patience
- it involves bearing evils and suffering with a tranquil mind

HUPOMONĒ stems from another Greek word, *HUPOMONŌ (G5278)*. This root word means:

- to stay under, to have fortitude
- to remain behind when others are gone
- to wait, to hold out

Review the key scripture again with these definitions in mind.

We are able to rejoice when problems arise because they spur learning. Challenges allow us to practice abiding in God with constancy, they force us to learn patience, they allow us to persevere through suffering and evil with tranquility of mind. Difficulties teach us to hold out, hold on, and have fortitude when we long to jump ship.

It is not fun to endure. To press on when mind and body revolt is grueling and painful. To learn patience is torturous, but to have patience is deep wealth. To learn to hold on is backbreaking, but to have persistence is a valuable commodity. To learn to reject worry is strenuous, but to have a tranquil mind is prized peace. The process of learning endurance is severe, but the fruit produced through training is a great harvest.

If you have a tendency toward being a doer, you may gear up at this point to try harder and be better at endurance. I caution you. Although endurance does require effort, this effort must be channeled toward knowing who God is and what He can do in us, rather than toward our ability to last longer or push harder. This is a critical difference! God is the One who equips us with this tenacity.

I spent years of my life failing to endure. I faced temptation, tried my best to resist, became preoccupied with my fragility, felt hopeless and discouraged, then conceded to sin. Again. And again. And again. I repeated this cycle so many times I'm provoked to nausea as I describe it to you. Despite extensive effort, I was never able to manufacture victory out of this cycle.

Instead, I was freed from this torment through a disparate cycle. Defeat lectured me often enough that I lost hope in my efforts. Fully persuaded I could not win, I cried out to One greater than me. Scripture instructed me to strain my mind and heart to fix on God's character and His actions. As I delighted in His presence with me even in the pit of temptation, God shifted my perspective from my fragility to His stability. He trained me in endurance, and moment by moment, gave me victory. In hindsight, I'm floored by how many moments of endurance have stacked up in this life of freedom He has enabled me to live.

A weird shift occurs when *trying to change* transforms into seeking God. When I clamored to be better, I set my sights on a goal like thirty days without falling, or one year without *that* sin, but I failed to come anywhere near. When all I could do is cry out to God with, "I need You now! And now! And now! Make my mind fix on You for the next sixty-seconds or three minutes," I was fashioned as an overcomer.

Have you experienced a similar cycle of *trying* which ended in defeat?

☐ Yes   ☐ No

If so, what is the hardest part of hearing instruction to endure? If not, what do you credit for your victory?

_____

_____

_____

Read the following scriptures and match them to the benefits of endurance (perseverance) listed below.

Scripture	Benefits of Endurance
James 1:4	Gain your lives
2 Peter 1:5-8	Receive what God promised
Hebrews 10:36	Be made mature and complete
Luke 21:19	Keep you from being ineffective and unproductive in your knowledge of the Lord

Scripture states there is a lot to gain through endurance. It promises those who endure will receive God's promises. We are also told we will gain our lives, be made mature and complete, and be kept from ineffective and unproductive knowledge of God. Endurance has a massive influence upon living by faith.

Character

The second quality said to be developed through trials in Romans 5:3-4, is *character*.

Character: DOKIMĒ (G1382)

The Greek word translated, character, is *DOKIMĒ*. The definition of this word has acute interest to me because it surprised me. The word signifies having experience, being tested, and being proven. It is derived from the Greek word *DOKIMOS (G1384)* which implies a state of being tried and proven genuine.

Character, therefore, refers to having experience, being tried and being proven genuine.

Record James 1:12.

_____

Similar to the key verse, this message connects the concepts of perseverance and character development. The words in the NIV say, "Having stood the test," but they are translated from the same root word we examined which denotes character, *DOKIMOS*. We are told God blesses the one who endures to the point of passing the test.

What blessing is promised?

_____

So, we see, trials allow us to grow in our ability to hold on, hold out, and remain steadfast in the Lord. As we endure through those trials with eyes fixed on Jesus, we develop character—that is, we are able to stand up in the test so there is proof of the genuineness of our faith.

When was the last time (or most significant time) you faced a substantial trial in your life?

_____

On the scale below, mark the extent to which you held fast to the Lord through that season.

1	5	10
Not at all	Partially holding to God	Held tightly to God

What evidence indicates you stood the test (ie. developed character as a result of your perseverance)?

_____

_____

_____

_____

What was hard about fixating on the Lord during the trial?

_____

_____

_____

_____

Hope

Going a step further, Romans 5:3-4 NLT pinpoints a connection between character and hope.

Fill in the blanks to track the progression in these verses.

Trials help us develop e _____ which proves our c _____ which strengthens our confident h _____ of salvation.

Hope: *ELPIS (G1680)*

The word translated, hope is, *ELPIS*. This means to anticipate with pleasure and to have a confident expectation of good. *ELPIS* also implies the presence of an object in whom the hope resides.

Okay, with endurance, character, and hope defined, we are ready to unpack this whole verse.

Difficulties propel us to persevere in faith, believing God will come through for us according to His character and actions. When we endure by fixing our eyes on God and His strength in us, our character is proven genuine. The development of character then, encourages us to anticipate good from the object in which we have hope.

Converse with God about the message of Romans 5:3-4. What do you think about God using challenges to develop endurance, character and hope in you? Please be authentic as you share with the Lord. Don't be afraid of mixed feelings—they are a sign of emotional maturity.

_____

_____

_____

_____

_____

_____

_____

_____

_____

Hope Causes a Shift in Focus

God is mysterious. I'm struck that while He allows trials to develop perseverance, character, and hope in us, He is hard at work ensuring something superior. To believe the ultimate goal is our improvement would be to miss the main point. You see, every aspect of what is meant to grow in us through trials, is based on God coming through for us in the way scripture says He will. The main point is not us coming through for God. The main point is us seeing proof that God will come through for us in our moments of greatest need. This doesn't dictate we get what we prefer, rather it promises God will adhere to His great character in all He does.

Trials come and we remain in the Lord with constancy (endure). We do this because God empowers us and helps us grasp who He is. As God assists us in endurance and we responsively press on, our character is proven genuine. More outstanding still, His character is proven genuine to us. In the midst of tests, we find proof we can remain because He is faithful to remain with us. Right in the middle of the end of ourselves, we discover we are upheld, and this makes for a fresh influx of faith.

Aware of God in and with us, we experience great hope! Hope for our present needs, but also hope for our future needs. The harvest hope grows in us is an assurance that transcends circumstances. Hope grows an anticipation of Him that deems future trials bearable.

This experiential knowledge of Him brings joy. Familiarity with God amidst our needs is the incredible prize won through endurance, character development, and hope. Growing faith is the logical response to being persuaded God is trustworthy, present, sustaining, and powerful. Our hope of salvation eternally, but also moment by moment, is proportionate to our confidence in Him who offers to save.

Take a look at the following verses and list the qualities of God that are highlighted in each.

Deuteronomy 7:9 _____

Psalm 86:15 _____

Jeremiah 32:17 _____

John 16:33 _____

1 Corinthians 10:13 _____

2 Thessalonians 3:3 _____

In light of these truths about God's character, how do you feel about your faith in Him? Do you desire to hold back or to go all-in with confident hope God will come through for you in accordance with who He is? Share your thoughts and feelings with God.

_____

_____

_____

_____

A Great Cloud of Witnesses

Key Verse

Hebrews 12:1-2 NIV: *"Therefore, since we are surrounded by such a great cloud of witnesses, let us throw off everything that hinders and the sin that so easily entangles. And let us run with perseverance the race marked out for us, fixing our eyes on Jesus, the pioneer and perfecter of faith."*

According to this verse, how can we know what it means to live by faith?

Witnesses

We have talked this week about how genuine faith is forged. Today, we will see this in action through stories of those who have gone before us, given to encourage us to thrive in faith. There are great, messy, wimpy, brave, doubt-filled people who have trudged along the roads we travel. Some were declared faithful by God and credited as righteous.

In the chapter preceding our key verse, the author of Hebrews urges us to understand what faith is, based on the lives of men and women who have gone before us.

Read Hebrews chapter 11. Circle the correct answer below.

1. According to Hebrews 11:1, faith is:
   a. to receive prophetic words from God
   b. to be confident of what we hope for
   c. to believe your gut-feeling is right
   d. to know that something is real even if we cannot see it
   e. both b and d

2. According to Hebrews 11:2, the ancient people who followed God were commended for what?
   a. keeping the law
   b. being excellent hunters
   c. faith
   d. humility
   e. both a and b

3. According to Hebrews 11:6, it is impossible to do what without faith in God?
   a. win the lottery
   b. heal people
   c. listen in church
   d. please God
   e. both b and c

4. Also according to Hebrews 11:6, what is necessary to come to God?
   a. belief that He exists
   b. belief that He will come to earth again
   c. belief that He is the creator of the world
   d. belief that He rewards those who seek Him
   e. both a and d

According to the stories listed in Hebrews 11, match the ancient believers listed below to their demonstration of faith in God.

Enoch (vs 5)	a. Offered a pleasing sacrifice to God
Noah (vs 7)	b. Considered God faithful to His promise that she would conceive even in old age
Abel (vs 4)	c. Prepared an ark to save his family in reverence to God
Abraham (vs 17-19)	d. Chose to endure ill treatment with the people of God rather than enjoy the passing pleasures of sin
Joseph (vs 22)	e. Considered God able to raise his son from death
Sarah (vs 11)	f. Did not see death because he was pleasing to God
Jacob (vs 21)	g. Spoke about the Israelites' exodus from Egypt and gave instructions about his burial
Moses (vs 24-25)	h. Worshipped God when he was in a season of dying

Beyond these heroes of faith are many more. In every case, faith was shown by the ways they endured, by the demonstration of their character in action, and by the hope they placed in the Lord despite the lack of proof supporting the outcomes they desired.

I want to caution you before we continue. There is a temptation when we look at the lives of others, to put them on unreachable pedestals. We can be lured to compare our mundane and lame moments with their spectacular moments. This trap can lead us to feel isolation and despair rather than encouragement. These witnesses were just as human and messy as you and I are today.

Moses had moments of doubt, frustration, and violence. Abraham and Sarah grew tired of waiting for God to come through on His promise for a son, so Abraham slept with his servant. Rahab was known as an immoral woman. The same Israelites who navigated the Red Sea begged to return to Egypt because they preferred the food.

God is not dependent upon perfection to utilize our faith. Even within the broken, less than pretty moments of believing, God can produce brilliance through our faith. When we believe in Him, place our trust in Him, and step out with hope in Him, we enter into the same realm of usability as those considered to be the great cloud of witnesses.

Week 1 *Faith Forges Ahead*

Take a step back to analyze the thoughts, feelings, and actions in your life. Where do you find evidence you trust in the Lord with confidence? Where do you find evidence you don't?

_____

_____

_____

_____

_____

_____

_____

_____

_____

Instructions for Endurance

The word translated as *never give up* in our key verse is the word, *HUPOMONĒ*, which we studied yesterday. We are to run the race of faith with endurance, remembering we will be changed as God proves Himself to us in our need.

Now read Hebrews 12:1-3 NIV to discover how we can do this. Fill in the blanks below.

1. Let us throw off everything that _____ and the _____ that so easily _____ . (vs 1)

2. Let us fix our eyes on Jesus, the pioneer and perfecter of _____ . (vs 2)

3. Consider Him, who endured such opposition from sinners, so that you will not grow _____ and lose _____ . (vs 3)

In your current season of life, what hinders you from running the race marked out for you? Does sin trip you up? Are there other webs entangling you?

_____

_____

_____

_____

What does it mean, in a practical sense, to fix your eyes on Jesus?

_____

_____

_____

_____

In Hebrews 11, we hear of people who were faithful, but in Hebrews 12:2, Jesus is elevated as the perfect prototype of faith. He is the inventor of faith, and He supplies powerful witness to life by faith.

What does it mean to you that Jesus demonstrated faith amidst His difficult experiences?

_____

_____

_____

_____

How is your sense of weariness impacted when you consider Jesus' trials and His triumphant seat with God?

_____

_____

_____

_____

If you are tired, discouraged, or weary, divulge your feelings to God.

_____

_____

_____

_____

Write out Hebrews 12:1-3 as a personalized prayer to God. To do this:
- **change the pronouns from we/us/you to I/me**
- **change the names and pronouns for God to the pronoun You**
- **take time to work through the verses in sincere conversation with God**

Here's an example of how to start:

Let's pray about this.

Lord, I am surrounded by such a great cloud of witnesses. Please equip me to throw off everything that hinders me and the sin that so easily entangles me. Let me throw off worry, let me throw off doubt, let me throw off…. (be specific).

Dive Deeper 1

· ·•· ● ·•· ·

Teach Me, O Lord

Write out Psalm 86:11-12 below.

_____

_____

_____

Pray for Readiness to Learn from God

┌─ *Example:* ─────────────────────────────────┐

Holy Spirit, You are with me. Every time I breathe, You are present. I can't do anything to produce Your fruit without You. Jesus promised He would send You so I could be taught. Please help me to learn from You. I want to learn. Search me and reveal anything that stands in the way of me hearing You, so I may confess and be free before You. Here I am, God. Please lead me, teach me, meet with me, wash me in Your love.

└───┘

You can pray along with this sample prayer or write one below to better communicate your thoughts and feelings.

_____

_____

_____

Listen and Confess

Be patient. Sit and wait before God. Listen to what rattles around in your mind and in your heart. Do you sense any conviction of sin, awareness of distraction, or impeding negativity? If so, confess these to God.

_____

_____

_____

_____

Review

With hindrances laid aside, ask God to lead you as you review the material from this week. Please do not skip this part, thinking you've already done the work. Learning to learn from God, to be open to His personal instruction, and to seek His voice are rich and deep blessings. I pray you will not settle for your experience of God to remain indirect, learning only through others. God will mentor you—what a thrill!

Write out the key scripture verse for each lesson this week. Then, highlight the main point you learned day by day. Make your reflections personal.

Day 1: Help My Unbelief

Mark 9:24

_____

_____

_____

Your Main Learning Point

_____

_____

_____

Day 2: More Precious Than Gold

1 Peter 1:7

_____

_____

_____

Your Main Learning Point

_____

_____

_____

Day 3: Endurance, Character, Hope

Romans 5:3-4

_____

_____

_____

Your Main Learning Point

_____

_____

_____

Day 4: A Great Cloud of Witnesses

Hebrews 12:1a

_____

_____

_____

Your Main Learning Point

_____

_____

_____

Study Skills

Which verse has been most impactful for you this week? It might be a key verse or perhaps a scripture embedded in a lesson spoke to you in a meaningful way.

Your Key Verse

_____

Paraphrase the verse so it communicates a sincere prayer to God. Allow the author's words to be a springboard for conversation with God about its content and your reflections. I'll use Hebrews 11:1 as an example.

> ### *Example*
>
> *Lord, faith shows confidence in what I hope for and assurance about what I do not see. Please grow this confidence in me. I know You may use trials or difficulties to mold me. You may require my endurance. You may build character in me, and give me confidence to place my hope in You whether I can see You at work or not. I surrender to You. Your process is trustworthy. I want You to build my faith. I am Yours.*

Re-write your key verse as a personalized prayer

_____

_____

_____

_____

_____

_____

_____

_____

Further Scripture Exploration

Choose a key word from the verse that drew your attention this week.

For example, the word that captivated my attention in Hebrews 11:1, was confidence.

Your Key Word

_____

Go to www.openbible.info/topics. Type this key word into the search bar and read the related verses.

Please note: **www.openbible.info/topics** is a user-generated site. Anyone can add verses to the topic pages (including you) so discernment is required. In dialogue with God, explore the relevance of these verses to what He is teaching you.

Write the references for those you discern as relevant, and make some notes about how you believe God is guiding you through them.

Reference   Relevance

_____   _____

_____   _____

_____   _____

_____   _____

Summarize what stands out to you in these verses.

_____

_____

Interact with God

Converse with God about your thoughts and feelings as you trust Him to lead you personally through His word. Do you have doubts? Do you feel thankful? Are you overwhelmed? Are you excited? Share your reflections with Him.

_____

_____

_____

_____

Ask God if specific obedience is required of you in response to what you have learned. Note what comes to mind.

_____

_____

_____

_____

Express to God your faith or lack of faith in Him as you respond to His instruction.

_____

_____

_____

_____

Week 2

THE POWER OF REVERENCE

Lesson 2

God Is

•••••

Head on over to www.lisadevries.ca/bigfreshfaith/
→ Watch the Video Lessons → Watch Lesson 2 and follow along below.

Jeremiah 10:7 ESV:

"Who would not _____ you, O King of the nations? For this is your due; for among all the wise ones of the nations and in all their kingdoms there is none like you."

•• You see, within the core struggles of faith, each of us has to decide,

who we are going to _____ as the greatest,

who we will _____ the most,

and who we are going to _____ in and through our lives.

•• The fingerprints of reverence can be seen in 4 things:

our view of God's _____ ,

our _____ on Him,

our _____ to His will, and

our _____ (or exaltation) of Him.

•• Jesus was _____ by the truth about God, He _____ Him completely,

and He was fully _____ God to come through in character and actions.

Hebrews 5:7 NLT:

"While Jesus was here on earth, he offered prayers and pleadings, with a loud cry and tears, to the one who could rescue him from death. And God heard His prayers because of His
_____ _____ for God."

•• Reverence positions us with our face fixed toward the _____ while we try to make

sense of our _____ , not our face set toward the _____ while we try

to make sense of our _____ .

•• Reverence shouts that who we are, what we think, and the circumstances we face

are _____ to the truth about God.

Suggestions for Prayer

- Talk to God about what stirs in you from this lesson.
- Throughout the week, ask God for opportunities to be reminded of His greatness and your relative position of smallness in comparison to Him.
- Thank God for being worthy of your reverence.

There is No One Like You

Key Verse

Jeremiah 10:6 NIV: *"No one is like you, Lord; you are great, and your name is mighty in power."*

Our study so far has shown that our faith involves trust and assurance in things not yet seen. God desires our faith be proven genuine, our character be proven genuine, and through our experience of God with us while we are tested, He will be proven genuine. Authentic faith gives us new life, new hope, and a new future. It secures for us a shield of God's power to endure our trials as it has for the faithful who have gone before us.

We've also uncovered that faith can be fraudulent when we claim to believe in God, give Him a superficial nod of trust, and yet are not willing to think, feel, or act in any way that expects God deliver what He says He will. God plans to be God to us, not treated like a powerless idol poised on the sidelines.

As we studied, faith is placed in someone or something. Faith is not faith by itself. By definition, faith demands an object in order to exist. As believers in Jesus Christ, the object of our faith is God. So, it stands to reason then, our faith is predicated upon our knowledge and perspective of who God is and what He does.

> As believers in Jesus Christ, our faith is predicated upon our knowledge and perspective of who God is and what He does. This makes accurate understanding of His character and actions imperative.

Understanding Reverence

Reverence means to fear, to be in awe, or to hold in high respect. Reverence is a response to something or someone. It is the reaction of fear, awe, and high regard that is present when the grand significance of someone or something is understood and experienced. Therefore, reverence for God is the fear, awe, and great respect that we feel in light of the grand significance of who God is and His position in relation to us. To better understand this concept, we will examine the following four things:

1. Our view of God's greatness

2. Our dependence upon Him

3. Submission to His will, and

4. Our worship of Him

We will tackle the first topic together today, while the others fill in the rest of this week's study. I want to challenge those of you who tend toward task orientation, or getting the "right" answers, to pause today and take time to reflect. You could buzz through this lesson and miss the opportunity to apply the material to your life. I believe God has something personal for each of us every time we study. Take time to seek Him when you face reflective questions. Remember, knowledge about God is all for naught, if not to impact our relationship with Him.

I. Our View of God's Greatness

The view we, as individuals, hold of God's significance and greatness will affect our experience of reverence toward Him. If we perceive God is feeble and weak, none of us would revere Him at all. On the other hand, if we perceive God is great, full of strength and power, and trustworthy to help us, we will revere Him tremendously.

I do not sit in awe over the mediocre. I do not hold in high respect the unimpressive. I need to be convinced God is someone to fear and hold in high regard, because the measure to which I revere Him correlates with the measure to which I trust Him. The view we have of God's greatness has a huge impact on our reverence for Him and the faith we place in Him.

Do you hold God in high regard? ☐ **Yes**   ☐ **No**

What do you know about Him that causes you to revere Him?

_____

_____

Read the following scriptures. Record your discoveries of God's greatness.

Psalm 86:8	_____	**Isaiah 44:6-8**	_____
Psalm 83:18	_____	**Isaiah 45:18**	_____
Psalm 86:10	_____	**2 Samuel 7:22**	_____
Psalm 135:5-6	_____	**Revelation 4:11**	_____

The God in whom we place our faith is no small God. He is the best, the biggest, and the One who is sovereign over every other existing being. He is worthy of our honor, praise, and glory. He does whatever He wants—no one controls Him. No one can contain Him.

Read 1 Chronicles 29:11 and 1 Samuel 2:2. If you believe these truths about God, then write the words out below as a personal expression of exaltation to God. If you struggle to believe these truths, then share that with Him in authentic prayer.

_____

_____

_____

_____

Does it impact you to read about the greatness of God? ☐ Yes ☐ No

Or is it so familiar that the topic of His majesty seems mundane? ☐ Yes ☐ No

Understanding God's greatness, and how that is relevant to you and I, is crucial to reverence and crucial to faith. Nonetheless, I have found it hard to come to grips with the notion of fear toward God because I am not afraid of Him. He's not like an intruder in my house, or an attacker coming toward me in a dark alley. You see, I trust God as merciful and loving, so I do not experience fear of Him in a malicious sense. With regard to reverence though, fear refers to something different. The fear of God refers to comprehension of the magnitude of who God is in relation to who I am. From that perspective, no doubt I am fearful of God.

Consider this example. Imagine inspecting the majesty of the largest, fastest plane at an airport. Imagine observing its size, hearing the auditory explosion of its jets, and watching as it lifts off the ground. No doubt you'd be impressed by its power.

Now imagine yourself standing in the middle of the runway as it comes in to land. You wouldn't be afraid in the sense of doubting its motives toward you, but you would certainly fear it in the sense of acknowledging it as bigger and more powerful than you. In this case, fear (reverence) would prescribe you get yourself off the runway. Your knowledge of the plane and its power causes you to revere it, and guides your behavior in accordance.

Fear of the Lord doesn't decree we question His motives and trustworthiness, rather, because we are aware of who He is and who we are in relation to Him, we give Him the right of way. I would not fight with a 747 over who ought to stand on the runway. The plane has the trump card. I move accordingly. Likewise, with the Lord—He is bigger, He is the boss.

Reflect on what God's superiority means to you. Why does it matter? If you find it difficult to connect with this, express that to God and ask Him to help you.

_____

_____

_____

_____

_____

_____

_____

_____

_____

_____

_____

Read the following scriptures and record all the benefits of reverence and/or the fear of the Lord.

Proverbs 9:10 _____   Psalm 34:9 _____

Proverbs 8:13 _____   Psalm 25:14 _____

Proverbs 19:23 _____   Luke 1:50 _____

Proverbs 14:26-27 _____

Reverence for God contributes to our faith because it acknowledges our position before Him, and His position as Lord of all. We need to know this to have any bit of freedom in our faith. If I put my life, my dreams, my loved ones, my vulnerability in someone else's hands, He'd better be bigger, better, and stronger than me! Otherwise such faith is foolishness!

Review the discoveries you made about God's greatness earlier in this lesson and the benefits of reverence listed above. Summarize what you have learned below.

_____

_____

_____

_____

_____

_____

Reverence for God stands in agreement with His power. It says, "You are bigger than me. You are better than me. You know more than me. I will live according to Your ideas and Your instructions." In this way, reverence halts self and yields to the power of God.

Express your thoughts, feelings, and questions about reverence to God.

_____

_____

_____

_____

_____

_____

Day 2

Apart From Me You Can Do Nothing

> ## Key Verse
>
> John 15:5 NIV: *"I am the vine; you are the branches. If you remain in me and I in you, you will bear much fruit; apart from me you can do nothing."*

Yesterday, the four aspects of reverence to be explored together this week were outlined. They are:

1. Our view of God's greatness

2. Dependence upon Him

3. Submission to His will

4. Worship of Him

Let's jump in with point number two.

2. Dependence Upon God

Dependence on God is based on two things.

1. My view of who God is and who I am in comparison

2. My view of what God can do and what I can do in comparison

If I believed I was capable of everything I ever longed for, God's superiority would not impact me with the significance it does when I understand I'm easily thwarted. Independence serves as a stumbling block to reverence. When I encounter my own limitations to the extent that I know for certain I need help from God, His superiority has a substantial impact on me. This dependence leads to reverence.

Read the key verse for our study today.

What are the conditions that precede fruit bearing?

_____

What are the conditions responsible for bearing nothing?

_____

Consider these examples.

1. Imagine a woman who has always had a steady income (either from her work or her husband's). This woman could credit the provision to: her skills, the fortitude of her husband's work ethic, the financial stability of her employer, or to God's sovereignty.

Whichever of these options she credits most, depends on, and believes to be most trustworthy is what she will most revere (fear, respect, hold in high regard). This object is what she will invest in if she is uncertain. The position of God high above any other power and in control of everything will impact this woman more if she experiences dependency on Him to provide, than if her default is to believe she can work it out on her own.

What/who do you believe is most trustworthy in providing for you? (Please avoid just saying God because you're trained to answer that way. Really think about it. Answer what is real and authentic for you.)

_____

_____

_____

2. Imagine a couple who has hit a rocky patch in their marriage. In order to move forward, they could place their trust in: their communication skills, their commitment to one another, a good counsellor, or in God to refine them.

    Whichever of these they place their trust in, is the object they will invest in. The truth that God is above all else will be impactful to the couple if their dependence is upon Him. If, instead, they are dependent upon their abilities or the abilities of others, God's greatness will seem irrelevant in their specific situation.

When you face difficulties in relationships, where do you lean?

_____

_____

_____

3. Imagine a woman who hasn't morally screwed up in any major way. She has made good choices, resisted temptation in the big areas, and her life is smooth. She could credit her righteousness to: a good upbringing, strong values, self-control, or God's grace.

    Given that she's a "good" Christian woman, she will know the right answer. In overt thought and word, she will give assent to God's grace, but the extent to which she believes that to be true and therefore depends on God moment by moment to help her through life, is the extent to which she will relish the majesty and superiority of God.

Do you find it difficult to relate to other's struggles? Are you frustrated by other's imperfections? To whom do you credit your apparent ability to avoid similar shortcomings?

_____

_____

_____

Dependency makes us aware that God's superiority is valuable to us. Independence causes us to dismiss God's superiority as irrelevant. Reverence, therefore, is associated with dependency on God in our specific circumstances. Critical to note, dependency on God does not mean it is wrong to use the abilities we have or to ask for help from other people when we need it. God absolutely uses these avenues to provide. Dependence on God acknowledges He is the maestro who equips us with our abilities, enlists the help of those around us as needed, and ensures we receive what He deems necessary for us.

This belief sits in contrast to the grossly independent society in which we live. We are inundated with messages telling us we ought to depend on ourselves. We are encouraged to believe that we have control, we organize our lives, we plan our future. In fact, I know many people who do not acknowledge dependence on God, yet seem to get along just fine. This can be disconcerting.

Do you question whether full-on dependency on God is necessary? Do you question whether it is worth it?

_____

_____

Ask God to reveal to you what your biggest hindrances are to dependency on Him. Consider the following list if you are unsure how to start. Put an x beside the conditions that challenge you.

___ **taking risks that require God to come through for you**

___ **believing He will care for you well**

___ **seeing where He is responsible for your success**

___ **trusting that what He provides is what you need**

Record any further insights below.

_____

_____

_____

_____

If you want to live with overt dependence on God, tell Him that. Ask for help where you find it difficult. Or, if you struggle to see why dependency on God is necessary or worth it, speak to Him about that instead.

_____

_____

_____

_____

Read the following scriptures. What are the benefits of dependence on God?

Philippians 4:13 _____

Isaiah 41:10 _____

Deuteronomy 4:20 _____

Ephesians 6:10 _____

Proverbs 3:5-6 _____

Psalm 33:20-22 _____

How do these benefits impact your desire to depend on God?

_____

_____

_____

_____

I did not hustle toward dependency on God. I meandered. I strolled. I drifted toward reliance on Him. That is, until He allowed me extensive trials. Then, I realized I was erudite in failure and guaranteed to fall flat on my face when self-dependent. I didn't learn this truth through a sermon at church, yet I'm sure it was preached. I became a John 15:5 savant by grappling with my precious loves and losing. Repeatedly. I used to believe dependency on anyone other than myself ensured loss, but the gospel truth is that dependency on God brings triumph through His power.

God does not tell us to trust in Him, wait on Him, rely on Him, and fear Him, so He can lord our neediness over us like a tyrant. He instructs us to depend on Him because He is bigger, better and stronger than we are. He necessitates dependence on Him because of who He is and what He can do. There is no one better to guide us, carry us, and provide for us. To be in His hands is to be in the best hands. He seeks the best for us.

Fruit

Your turn to consider the key verse, John 15:5.

Jesus' statement about fruit refers to proof of His Spirit inside us. That is, fruit (or acts empowered by the Holy Spirit) serve as external indicators of a divine internal dwelling. Jesus intends to use our dependence on Him to reveal Himself to the world. We cannot testify in truth without the Holy Spirit, no matter how hard we try. Christ wasn't stating an option for better life performance, He was stating an unavoidable fact.

Read John 15:5-11.

What is the consequence of not remaining in Jesus (i.e. living independent of Him)? (vs 6)

_____

What is the benefit of Jesus' words remaining in you (i.e. depending on His truth)? (vs 7)

_____

What is the purpose of bearing fruit? (vs 8)

_____

What specifically are you told to remain in? (vs 9)

_____

How is that accomplished? (vs 10)

_____

What is the personal benefit of this instruction to remain in (depend on) Jesus? (vs 11)

_____

Jesus knows we are happier in His hands. He knows we benefit when we depend on His love, because He knows He is 100% trustworthy. There is no one better equipped to take care of us!

Have you felt John 15:5 to be true in experience?

_____

_____

Talk to God about His desire for your dependence. Wrestle with any doubts you have about His purpose in this. Confess any independence uncovered throughout this lesson. Thank Him for the benefits He extends to you when you depend on Him.

_____

_____

_____

_____

_____

_____

_____

_____

_____

_____

Give Yourself Completely to God

┌─ *Key Verse* ──

James 4:7a EXB: *"So, give yourselves completely [submit] to God."*

└─────────────────────────────────────── · ·●●●· · ─

3. Submission to His Will

The third factor for us to explore this week in regard to the power of reverence, is submission.

Read James 4:1-7. Summarize what the message is in these verses.

_____

_____

_____

_____

When we allow our selfish desires and personal bents to guide our actions, we are arrogant and self-dependent. Jesus' brother, James, urges us to align with God's motives and will, and to turn away from the ways of the world.

Submission: HUPOTASSŌ (G5293)

As used in James 4:7, submission is the act of laying down one's will for another's. It stems from the word HUPOTASSŌ, which signifies one person allowing himself to become subject to another, to be in obedience to another. Submission involves giving oneself completely to be in subjection to another.

To discuss submission today, we will break it down into two parts. The first is the act of the soul in surrender to the will of God, and the second is the resulting obedient thoughts, feelings, and actions.

> • **Surrender**

Read Matthew 26:36-46. Answer the questions below.

How did Jesus feel about carrying out His Father's will? (vs 37-38)
>   a. excited to fulfill this plan
>   b. scared for His life
>   c. grieved to the point of death

What did Jesus pray for 3 times? (vs 39,42,44)

_____

_____

There were many excruciating moments in Jesus' life; however, I think the moments recorded in this passage are at the top of the list. Here in this garden, we are permitted to witness Jesus' surrender to the Father's will, even though His voracity was to have this one pass.

Although Jesus was God, He took on human flesh, which included all the associated tumult and pain. He understood the magnitude of what lay ahead of Him and He was emotionally distraught.

Read this same story in Luke 22:39-46.

Jesus was in need of support. What support did He ask for? (vs 40)

_____

What support did God send? _____ **Why?** _____ **(vs 43)**

Jesus was in _____ **. His sweat was like drops of** _____ **. (vs 44)**

This was no easy moment for Jesus. This was perhaps the most pivotal moment of His life. He wrestled with His human desires, He asked for help, and He was strengthened at God's command. Jesus surrendered to God's will and endured in the face of suffering. Through this, He gave us a beautiful depiction of the surrender necessary in submission.

No surprise at this point, I'm sure...submission has been painstaking for me. I never like being told what to do. When presented with one "right" way to do something, I think, "I wonder how else it could be done?" I don't set out to be difficult, but I find the diversity in most situations causes me a reflexive response to reject absolutes. This is, of course, unless I discover them to be true through my own experience. My compulsive need to get my hands in the mud is both a strength and a dreadful weakness. Sometimes it helps in problem solving, but other times it sources colossal mistakes. I chastise myself to heed wisdom from others, yet I rarely comply.

I went to a Shakespearian play once called, *The Taming of the Shrew*. Bard on the Beach, as the outdoor theatre in Kitsilano, BC, is known, left a lasting imprint. The story was about a stubborn and independent woman named Kate. She was reluctant to heed authority, let alone the rule of obnoxious, Petruchio, who had become her husband. Petruchio set out to tame Kate and by the end of the play, Kate accepts the power and benefit of submission to him. I'm sure that is not a great description of the full scope of the play, but it's what has stuck in my mind because of the heightened sense of conviction I experienced while watching.

I was, at that time, deep in a place of rebellion toward God. I knew who God was, I believed in Him, but I did not revere Him. I was not willing to acknowledge my dependence upon Him, and did not want to surrender to His will. In fact, at the time, I couldn't comprehend how to surrender to His will.

As I watched the play, the Holy Spirit shouted to my heart as though through a megaphone. Every time Kate fought Petruchio and forced her will, I cringed at the resemblance to myself. As her stubbornness incited backlash, I reflected on my life and my stomach turned. In the end, when she figured

Have you ever felt like the Holy Spirit is trying to get your attention, yet been unwilling to listen? Do you know what held you back from surrender?

out Petruchio was for her, not against her, I registered God's assurance that surrender was not synonymous with harm.

I'd like to tell you this led to instant transformation, but it didn't. Instead it haunted me, bothered me, irritated me, while I continued in my lack of submission. I travelled this road to a point where I had no choice but to cry out to God because everything else I had placed my faith in had crumbled around me. I encountered my weakness and depravity and could deceive myself no longer.

Truth percolated through my experiences. I needed a Savior who exceeded me. God's identity as great, holy and powerful drew me to Him. My reverence for Him developed as my view of myself diminished. My dependence on Him advanced as my failure made independence ludicrous. Slowly, my surrender to Him matured as I accepted that He is better for me than any other plan I could muster.

To learn these concepts brought agony, but in order to lay down my will for God's, significant taming had to occur. My arrogant and rebellious heart was a barrier to the reverence required to be in step with God.

For me, change occurred because as I experienced desperation, God allowed me to catch glimpses of His love, grace and majesty. He began to show me, firsthand, who He is, and in the absence of arrogance, I hungered for more of Him. He took my yoke of self-slavery and replaced it with His yoke of God-reliance.

Ask God to reveal any stumbling blocks to your submission. Record what comes to mind below.

_____

_____

_____

_____

_____

_____

_____

_____

_____

Holding God in high regard is tied to His greatness. Without who He is, our devotion would be ridiculous. Reverence stems out of an acknowledgment of our inferiority to God and thus, fuels surrender and obedience.

- **Obedience**

Go back and read Matthew 26:46 again.

Jesus says, "Rise! Let us go! Here comes my betrayer!" Jesus submitted to God. He surrendered His will to God's in the garden, then put the sentiment of His heart into action by doing what God sent Him to do.

Jesus demonstrated that submission cannot stop short of obedience or it is not submission at all. He affirmed that when we choose submission in the hardest things, victories are won. Triumphs not just for Jesus, but for the one doing the submission also.

Read James 4:7-10. Read the summary of victories that follow the instruction to submit to God. Check the ones you would like to experience in your life.

___ Successful resistance of the devil

___ Being near to God

___ God being near to you

___ Being washed from sin

___ Being purified from double-mindedness

___ Experiencing a merited change in feelings toward sinful behavior

___ Having humility before God

___ Being lifted up by God

Ask God for victory in these specific areas, or in any others that you desire.

_____

_____

_____

_____

_____

Read Luke 6:46-49.

Obedience matters to God. Not because He is an egomaniac who gets a kick out of controlling us. Obedience matters to God because He wants us to be steady on His foundation when troubles come. He desires to provide us with safety and security, but to do so requires we obey Him. In the same way, we chide our children not to play in the street because we love them and want to protect them, Jesus instructs us. Obedience is not about God stamping a limit on our fun; it is about Him giving us life.

Notice the contrast between verses 48 and 49. In the first, the winds come and the house remains secure. In the second, the house collapses and is obliterated. God does not plan destruction for us! His guidelines are like those any loving parent gives. God steers us to obey for our safety, for our joy, and because He is more knowledgeable and wise than us.

What are your thoughts and feelings about giving yourself completely to God? Talk to God in honesty about these reflections.

_____

_____

_____

_____

_____

_____

Spiritual Act of Worship

┌─ *Key Verse* ──────────────────────────────────┐

Matthew 4:10b NIV: *"Worship the Lord your God, and serve Him only."*

└──────────────────────────────── ··●●●·· ─┘

In review, we have learned reverence for God is intertwined with acknowledgment of His greatness, dependence upon Him, and submission to His will. We have seen there are many benefits to revering God— wisdom, peace, joy, power and purpose, to name a few.

Today, we will highlight how reverence propels us to worship God. Without reverence, God is not worshipped. Let's dive into this concept of worship and see how it is born out of reverence.

4. Our Worship of Him

Before I teach, let me ask you a question. What defines worship? Write your thoughts below.

_____

_____

If you asked me this question before I studied worship, I would've said it is the act of praising and thanking God for who He is. I would've said it was the exercise of celebrating the character and actions of God—applauding Him, raving about Him, focusing my attention on Him and all His splendor. Is that what you wrote too?

In church, the terms, *praise and worship,* are spoken together so commonly I assumed they were the same thing. In research, I discovered they have distinction. To give God praise is part of worship. To worship includes thoughts, feelings, and actions that expand beyond praise.

Praise refers to thinking or speaking about God with admiration. Thankfulness partners with praise when applauding God causes us to reflect on how His awesomeness impacts us as individuals. In scripture, praise and thanksgiving are often accompanied by music and song.

Here are some scriptures that speak of praise and thankfulness. Read them and note the correlated behavior.

Psalm 150:1-6 _____

Hebrews 13:15 _____

Acts 16:25 _____

Psalm 95:1-5 _____

Psalm 115:1 _____

Thankfulness and expressions of praise are imperative to worship, but they fall short in capturing the full extent of the concept. To grasp the depth, let's look at two further aspects together.

1. Bowing before God
2. Serving God

• **Bowing Before God**

Matthew 4 records the forty-day journey of Jesus into the desert where He was tempted by satan. The enemy's last pitch to Jesus was to offer Him all the kingdoms of the world if He bowed down to worship him. In verse 10, Jesus quotes Deuteronomy 6:13, "Worship the Lord [our] God, and serve Him only."

Read the following scriptures. As you do, jot down what these verses teach you with regard to worship.

Psalm 95:6-7 _____

Exodus 20:5 _____

2 Chronicles 20:18 _____

Worship: SHÂCHÂH (H7812)

Each use of the word, *worship,* in the references above stems from the same Hebrew word. *SHÂCHÂH* is defined as to bow down, to fall prostrate, to do reverence, and it implies the object is deserving of this show of homage.

Worship stems out of reverence because reverence examines God's greatness, acknowledges His position of superiority over us, and causes us to fall on our face before Him. We bow down in a show of our relative position and powerlessness before God. To bow down is a lone outward action, but the intention to communicate subservience is what imparts the action with significance.

Note the responses of faithful people who have gone before us when encountering the Lord.

Revelation 1:17 _____

Ezekiel 3:23 _____

Numbers 22:31 _____

Exodus 3:4-6 _____

1 Kings 19:11-13 _____

Each of these people encountered God and responded with worship. They were not full of words, they were speechless, in awe, bowed down, overwhelmed. This expression is meant by the word, worship, in our key verse. The Greek word used for worship in the key verse is *PROSKUNEŌ,* (G4352). This echoes this expression of prostrating oneself in homage and adoration.

Have you ever experienced God in such a way you felt compelled to prostrate yourself before Him? If so, describe that situation.

_____

_____

_____

_____

If not, would you like to encounter God in such a way? Why or why not?

_____

_____

_____

_____

I am not an exuberant person. I am more introvert than extrovert. I shy away from attention unless in my safest places. There is no part of me that desires to bow down before God as a show. But in the privacy of my relationship of God, I am hungry for as much of Him as I can stand. I want God to reveal His glory to me and to flatten me with His majesty.

Despite desire, settling into worship can sometimes be a struggle. I can be tempted to trade a few songs for genuine awe. Other times, I have issues with God, feel angry toward Him, or experience resentment over His sovereign decisions. Such challenges can interrupt my passion to worship Him. It takes time and intention to meditate on God when our minds are preoccupied with so much else.

What are some of the things that stand in your way of bowing down before God?

_____

_____

_____

- **Serving God**

The second aspect of worship on our agenda today is the concept of service to God.

Read the following scriptures. Note any clues that link the idea of worship to service.

Exodus 4:23 _____

Joshua 24:15,18 _____

Psalm 2:11 _____

The word translated as *worship* or *serve* in each of these verses is *ÂBAD* (H5647). This word has a different meaning than to bow down in awe. The idea is to work for, to serve, or to be compelled. Used in relation to serving people, it implies toilsome labor. Used in the sense of being compelled to serve God, it has a unique flavor that associates a joyful experience of liberation with the action of serving.

Surprising, right? Maybe like me, you failed to see how strong the connection is between acknowledging God for who He is and serving Him. Please, please, don't get misled here by the idea of legalistic servitude. There is no room for obligatory drudgery in worship! It is an impossible progression of events.

Imagine coming face to face with the Lord's majesty. Imagine an encounter so potent you can do nothing but fall facedown before Him. The next link in this progression can't sidestep to, "Oh great, I guess You expect me to serve You—what a drag." That would be absurd. Imagine the sheer privilege to do anything for the Lord. An undeserved joy. I picture myself enthralled with the Lord, afraid to look up but unable to keep my eyes off Him. If He invited me to serve Him, I would be overwhelmed, honored and eager as can be.

> Imagine coming face to face with the Lord's majesty. Imagine falling face down before Him. Imagine God asking you to talk to someone on His behalf. Would this seem like a burden or privilege to you?

Read Romans 12:1 NIV and fill in the blanks below.

"I urge you, brothers and sisters, in view of God's mercy, to offer your bodies as _____ _____ , holy and pleasing to the Lord— this is your true and proper _____ ."

Worship: LATREIA (G2999)

The Greek word translated here as *worship*, is *LATREIA*. This word, used to refer to God and priests, suggests services rendered either for hire or due to enslavement.

Either way, we are urged by Paul to offer ourselves as living sacrifices in the same way the priests made offerings to the Lord in the temple. We are to be given to the Lord for the purpose of non-negotiable service. This is worship.

I love music, and I love music in church. I love praising God alone, and I love to express thankfulness corporately with the body of Christ in my community. I cherish both of these essential modes of worship. However, if I think by keeping time with the song leader, I fulfill God's command to worship Him, I conclude in error. My life of worship must extend beyond what can take place in fifteen minutes on a Sunday. Worship is designed to penetrate mind, heart and soul.

Describe your current experience of worship?

_____

_____

_____

_____

Is there anything you would like to change (even if you don't know how to change it)? Talk to God about these thoughts and feelings. Ask Him for help.

_____

_____

_____

_____

I hope you are as excited as I am about how these concepts flow in and out of one another. Despite all my wrestling to come in line with it, I believe reverence is beautiful. It acknowledges who God is and accepts our dependency on Him. It calls us to submit to God both in surrender and in obedience. Incredibly, it equips us to worship God—in terms of bowing down before Him, and being delighted to serve Him. Reverence is a state of awe, dependence, and surrender. It is a call to obey and serve Him as our spiritual act of worship.

Dive Deeper 2

Comfort Me, O God

Write out Matthew 11:28-30 below.

_____

_____

_____

_____

_____

_____

_____

_____

Pray for Readiness to Learn from God

Example

Lord, You invite me to take Your yoke upon me. You tell me I can learn from You. I want You to teach me, God. You promise You are gentle and humble in heart, and as I obey You in this, I will find rest for my soul. Please God, fulfill this promise to me. I am asking that You equip me to learn from You personally and from Your word. You can do it! I trust You to come through in this.

You can pray along with this sample prayer or write one below that better communicates your thoughts and feelings.

_____

_____

_____

_____

Listen and Confess

Ask God if there is anything in your life that might stand in the way of hearing from Him today. Be patient. Sit and wait before God. Listen to what rattles around in your mind, and in your heart. Do you sense any conviction of sin, awareness of distraction, or impeding negative feelings? If so, confess your attachment to those things, and ask God to remove them.

_____

_____

_____

_____

_____

_____

Review

With these hindrances laid aside, ask God to lead you as you review the material from this week. Please do not skip this part, thinking you've already done the work. Learning to learn from God, learning to be open to His personal teaching, and learning to seek His voice is a rich and deep blessing. I pray you will not settle for God to only teach you indirectly, through others. God can teach you directly! It is such a thrill!

Write out the key scripture verse for each lesson this week. Then, highlight the main point you learned day by day. Make your reflections personal. This may be different for each person. There is not one right answer.

Day I: There is No One Like You

Jeremiah 10:6

_____

_____

_____

Your Main Learning Point

_____

_____

_____

Day 2: Apart from Me You Can Do Nothing

John 15:5

_____

_____

_____

Your Main Learning Point

_____

_____

_____

Day 3: Give Yourselves Completely to God

James 4:7a

_____

_____

_____

Your Main Learning Point

_____

_____

_____

Day 4: Spiritual Act of Worship

Matthew 4:10b

_____

_____

_____

Your Main Learning Point

_____

_____

_____

Interact with God

Spend some time practicing reverence for God.

God's Greatness: Acknowledge to God the truths you learned about Him this week.

_____

_____

_____

_____

Dependence on God: Express to God what you have learned about your dependence upon Him.

_____

_____

_____

_____

Submission to God: Ask God if there is anything He wants you to surrender to Him. If so, wrestle through this with Him, and walk it out in obedience.

_____

_____

_____

_____

Worship God: Bow your heart and mind before God. Present yourself to Him as a living sacrifice. Ask Him what He requires of you today.

_____

_____

_____

_____

Week 3

INTIMATE
PRESENCE

Intimate Acquaintance

••●••

Head on over to www.lisadevries.ca/bigfreshfaith/
→ Watch the Video Lessons → Watch Lesson 3 and follow along below.

Psalm 139:1-4 NASB:

"O Lord, You have searched me and known me. You know when I sit down and when I rise up; You understand my thought from afar. You scrutinize my path and my lying down, and are _____ _____ with all my ways. Even before there is a word on my tongue, behold, O Lord, You know it all."

Profitability & Reciprocal Relationship

••• God's intimate acquaintance signifies He will use His knowledge about you to _____ to you in a manner that is _____ for you.

••• He uses His intimate acquaintance to minister in a way that is _____ —not with riches and fame—but profitable in spirit and in eternity.

••• We must never lose sight of the fact that Christ's intimate ministry is of use, service, _____ , and _____ to us!

••• Experiencing God means participating with Him in a _____ relationship.

••• When relating with God, we must check out our experiences against what _____ says is true about God, and we must exercise _____ to guard against making idols of our preferences or perspectives.

••• Not devoid of discernment, _____ God in relationship is imperative to forging faith.

Suggestions for Prayer

• Talk to God about what stirs in you from this lesson.

• Ask for the Holy Spirit to bring to mind examples of how God has used His intimate knowledge of you to minister to you in a manner that was beneficial for you.

• Throughout the week, ask God for opportunities to minister on His behalf in a manner that profits His plans, His people, and His kingdom.

• Thank God for His willingness to be in an intimate and reciprocal relationship with you.

To Seek and Be Sought

· •● ● ●• ·

— Key Verse —

Jeremiah 29:13 NIV: *"You will seek me and find me when you seek me with all your heart."*

Last week we explored the power of reverence. We learned four aspects essential to faith.

Can you remember what they are?

1. _____ 2. _____

3. _____ 4. _____

I hope the truth of God's beauty has impacted your reliance, your submission and your worship this week. I hope your study of His character and actions has brought freedom in some tangible way—freedom to trust, step out, love, give, or stop when stopping was needed. I feel comradery with you in your journey.

Reverence is formed out of an acknowledgment of God's greatness, our smallness in comparison, and the resulting dependence we have upon Him. Given this acknowledgment, reverence then leads to submission and worship. My prayer is that each of us has new excitement about revering God in mind, heart and action.

This week, our attention shifts to a second essential component of faith—intimacy. Intimacy is a word used to describe a variety of experiences in our culture. It is used to indicate privacy and exclusivity in relationships. It expresses a deep sense of emotional sharing and familiarity. It can also refer to sexual relations, though of course not when we're talking about our relationship with God.

To discover the importance of intimacy with God, we will explore three actions of intimacy. My hope is for you to discover the beauty of intimacy with God with newness and openness. I also feel cautious toward the difficulty of this topic for some. Please know I have prayed for you at length. I continue to plead with God for healing and freedom from any damage our culture has done to you around this topic.

Express to God your feelings about discovering greater intimacy with Him.

_____

_____

_____

_____

Three Actions of Intimacy

Throughout our studies this week, we will look into three actions of intimacy. These are:

1. To Seek and Be Sought
2. To Know and Be Known
3. To Love and Be Loved

To Seek and Be Sought

Today, we begin by exploring the significance of seeking God and being sought by God.

- **To Seek God**

Read the key verse for today, Jeremiah 29:13.

God desires His people to seek Him and He promises when they do, they will find Him.

The same verse in *The Message* highlights the fervency of seeking and the promise of satisfaction in finding God.

> *Jeremiah 29:13 MSG - "When you come looking for me, you'll find me. Yes, when you get serious about finding me and want it more than anything else, I'll make sure you won't be disappointed. God's Decree."*

The same point is also stated to the Israelites in Deuteronomy 4:29. In this instance, the Israelites were in a state of rebellion against God, and God was about to scatter them among the nations. God, however, shared that His goal was for the Israelites to turn back to Him. Read Deuteronomy 4:29 to hear God's promise to them.

Considering Jeremiah 29:13 and Deuteronomy 4:29, how are we supposed to seek God?

_____

_____

_____

To Seek: BĀQASH (H1245) & DĀRASH (H1875)

There are two Hebrew words that translate into seek in both these verses. In each, the first time seek appears it is the word, *BĀQASH* which means to search out, to strive after, to desire and enquire. Through this word, God instructs His people to search Him out and strive after Him with desire. The second time the word seek appears, the word *DĀRASH* is utilized. The word has a connotation of continuousness—to frequent, to follow in pursuit to worship.

Together then, God guides us to search for Him and He promises to be found when we pursue Him with awe and servitude.

The two components of seeking are:

    1. BĀQASH: To _____ Him out, to _____ after, to desire

    2. DĀRASH: To seek continuously, to frequent, to follow in _____
        to worship

Let's look into this further. Read the following scriptures, and note how we ought to seek God.

1 Chronicles 16:11 _____

Proverbs 8:17 _____

Psalm 119:10 _____

Psalm 63:1 _____

God intends us to seek Him continually, diligently, and with our full hearts. He instructs us to thirst after Him like people who are desperate for water.

Do you know this kind of seeking?   ☐ Yes   ☐ No

Describe your experience.

_____

_____

_____

_____

_____

To seek God with continuance and diligence, one must be convinced she needs Him in and through her life. She must know that if she fails to seek Him, decompensation awaits. Uncomfortable truth to get to, yet a beautiful one to know.

I remember a time when I experienced a deep betrayal. Blind-sided, I staggered around. Like from the sting of a bullet ant, I was riveted by pain. At any moment of any day my mind was consumed. No amount of thought, analysis or new information relieved the incessant hunger for more thinking, analyzing, and investigating. No matter how long I ran on the hamster wheel, escape from the shock, heartbreak, and bewilderment eluded me.

The powerlessness over my mind and heart drove me to seek God in ways I never had before. I cried out to God and begged Him to equip me to focus on Him. Only in those moments I felt I could breathe. I was forced by the torment within to seek Him continually, with certain diligence, and to surrender of every ounce of my own heart. I was parched—Sahara Desert kind of parched—in every moment of every day for a long time.

It was here, in this ugly place, my knowledge of His intimate presence deepened. I cherished the dependency-driven search for Him because, in doing so, I found Him. Can you imagine a greater treasure? I have never come upon a drink that compares to the elation of finding His living water when I'm about to die of thirst.

No one desires to live in such a constant state of wreckage—I certainly do not. I can now call the season to mind and my heart remains at rest, but the journey to heal was complicated and can't be underestimated. The greatest take away from the incessant torment was the bounty of incessant desire for God.

I hunger for Him when I wake up at 6 am, when I read His word at 8, when I sit with clients as a counsellor throughout the day, when I tell others about Him, when I coach sports, when I tuck my kids into bed at night, when I relax with my husband at the end of the day. All the time, I crave to see God, to find Him in the mix, to catch a glimpse of His glory around me. Don't you just ache for Him?

Re-read Jeremiah 29:13 and Deuteronomy 4:29. What is the benefit promised to us when we seek God absolutely?

_____

Such good news, isn't it?

To Find: MÂTSÂ (H4672)

The promise to *find*, in these verses stems from the Hebrew word *MÂTSÂ*. In context, it communicates God will come forth, He will appear and be present. My favorite part is it also implies we embrace Him in the sense of holding to Him. I love this definition because it suggests as He appears and reveals Himself, we will be able to take hold of Him. Not to control Him, but rather to grasp, to comprehend and to be satisfied by Him. To my ears, it's a delightful notion.

Read the following scriptures and note the other benefits available to us when we seek God.

Lamentations 3:25 _____

Psalm 34:10 _____

Psalm 9:10 _____

2 Chronicles 7:14 _____

Jeremiah 33:3 _____

There is so much to discover when we seek God. As He is found by us, He reveals Himself to us. We find not only God with us, but His good, compassionate, sustaining, non-forsaking character as well. To seek God leads to great richness and deep satisfaction.

• To Be Sought by God

We are urged to seek God with abandon, but the gracious God whom we seek does not ask us to do that which He, Himself, has not already done. God seeks us through all time. In creation, in the garden of Eden, in the fall of man, in the history of the Israelites, in the welcoming of the Gentiles, in the life, death, and resurrection of Christ, in the coming of the Holy Spirit, in the ministry of the disciples, in the launching of the church, in the body of believers, and in the promise of future glory, God reveals His presence and His pursuit of His cherished creation.

Read John 6:44. How do we begin to seek God?

- "No one can come to me unless the Father who sent Me _____ them."

Read the following scriptures about God's intention to relate with us. Resist the urge to breeze over the verses due to their familiarity. Please allow them to fall fresh as you consider them through the lens of God's intention to intimately seek you.

- Romans 3:23 —> John 14:6 —> Romans 5:8 —> 1 John 1:9 —> Ephesians 2:13

Summarize the scriptural truths as related to God's intent to seek a relationship with you.

_____

_____

_____

_____

_____

_____

God planned and implemented our salvation for the purpose of relationship. To save us from sin was to reconcile us in relationship to God. Unable to offer God anything of value, we are dependent on God for restoration. Thankfully, he pursues an intimate relationship with us. So much so, He suffered to the max to remove every hindrance. Without His journey to the cross and His resurrection, seeking Him would never result in finding Him. In His great mercy, He endured so we could be satisfied. How great a Savior we have!

Does the extent to which Jesus pursued a relationship with you impact your desire to seek Him with genuine longing? Please don't say yes on autopilot here. Think it through. If there is a disconnect for you between Jesus' actions and your own, please be honest about it. Intimacy with God is fostered through authenticity.

_____

_____

_____

_____

_____

_____

Talk to God about your thoughts and feelings in relation to His pursuit of you and your pursuit of Him.

_____

_____

_____

_____

_____

_____

To Know and Be Known

····•·●·•····

John 10:14 NIV: *"I am the good shepherd; I know my sheep and my sheep know me."*

Yesterday we learned that intimacy develops with God through reciprocal seeking. God sought a relationship with us and He promises if we seek a relationship with Him, we will not be disappointed. This is such good news!

Today, we explore a second concept related to intimacy development—reciprocal knowing. Our key verse may be familiar to many of you. Let's take a minute to pray for new learning even in this well-known scripture.

Read Hebrews 4:12 and pray along with me.

Lord, Your word is alive and active. Your Spirit teaches as we read it with expectation to hear from You. Please take this familiar passage and penetrate each of us today. Your word has power to impact our hearts, minds, and deepest joints and marrow. Have Your way with us, Lord.

2. To Know and Be Known

Read the key scripture for today.

Know: GINŌSKŌ (G1097)

The word know, in this verse is the Greek word *GINŌSKŌ*. It means to know in a completed sense. It means to have knowledge of something or someone with the idea of volition or goodwill. This kind of knowing means to approve or to love, essentially to care for. The key verse suggests, then, that Jesus has full knowledge of us and approves, loves, and cares for us. It also states that those who follow Him like sheep, have a completed knowing of Him which responsively allows us to reflect similar love and care for Him.

How does Jesus identify Himself in our key verse?

_____

_____

Jesus explains the actions of a shepherd in the previous part of the chapter.

Read John 10:1-15, and record the actions for which the shepherd and the sheep are responsible.

Actions of the Shepherd	Actions of the Sheep
_____	_____
_____	_____
_____	_____
_____	_____
_____	_____
_____	_____

Jesus, as our Shepherd, has many responsibilities. He is identified as the Shepherd not by a big sign in flashing lights that announces His position, but rather, He is known by the sheep as their Shepherd by how He cares for them. This demonstrates that the Shepherd's knowing in a complete sense, is linked with loving and caring, which in turn allows the sheep to know and love the Shepherd. There is reciprocity in this knowing, but it is initiated and made possible for the sheep by the Shepherd.

The actions of the sheep in response are clear. Because of the Shepherd's knowledge, love, and care, the sheep listen to His voice, know His voice, and follow His voice. In these actions, they demonstrate they completely know and love the Shepherd.

It is also crucial to recognize in the midst of this reciprocal knowing, there is opposition.

Review John 10:1-15 one more time. List the actions of the antagonists (the thief, robber, stranger, and hired hand) and the actions of the sheep in response to their opposition.

Actions of the Opposition	Actions of the Sheep
_____	_____
_____	_____
_____	_____
_____	_____
_____	_____

The antagonists try to trick the sheep to follow them to steal, kill, and destroy the sheep. Should the opposition successfully lead the sheep astray, they will bail at the first sign of danger, because they care nothing for the sheep. Brutal enemies, the opposition desires to do devastating harm, and their interests are purely selfish.

The sheep, those who know and follow the Shepherd, will run away from the sound of a voice that is foreign. They will not listen to it. Their best defense against being led astray is to recognize the voice is not the Shepherd's, and to flee from it.

Do you hear the importance of knowing the Shepherd in this? The sheep are not kept safe by knowing all about the thief, robber, stranger, and hired hand. They are kept safe by knowing the Shepherd! It is the full knowledge of who the Shepherd is, the sound of His voice, and the experience of His love and care, that equip the sheep to respond appropriately. The right response is to flee from everyone and everything pretending to be the Shepherd.

> Do you know how to distinguish the Shepherd's voice from the enemy's? Do you know with certainty who God is and what He promises to do for you?

I recently watched a video put out by the Bank of Canada to help raise awareness about counterfeit money. The video did not show a single counterfeit bill. The whole film was focused on the details of real money. With regard to our Canadian polymer notes, emphasis was placed on the subtly raised letters and slightly raised edges around the portrait. It described the two transparent windows, and the details of the images within each.

I have spent Canadian money for a long time. I'm familiar with it. I like how it feels in my hands and I like what it allows me to do. But I didn't have any idea how to distinguish real money from counterfeit and never noticed several features on the bills.

I wonder how often this is true for us as believers. We've heard about God for a long time. We are familiar with the stories about Him. We like how it feels to connect in church, or pray in the moments of desire or need. Sadly though, we overlook His features and know with more certainty what He can do for us than the trademarks of His character. The tragedy is not only that we fail to know our Shepherd, also we are powerless to recognize the enemy and flee from him.

Read 2 Corinthians 10:5 NIV and fill in the blanks below.

"We _____ arguments and every pretension that sets itself up against the _____ of God, and we take _____ every thought to make it obedient to _____."

We are encouraged to protect our knowledge of God. We first need to know God, be familiar with His voice, and be active in following Him. Then, if any opposition comes, we take it captive to make it obedient to Christ.

In the sheep analogy, if a little sheep is in the pasture and something he doesn't recognize as the Shepherd approaches, the sheep flees, runs to the Shepherd he loves, and checks out the foreign element with Him. Then, the sheep submits to the authority of the Shepherd over that element. Remember, the Shepherd is trusted and approved. If He says it's the work of the thief, robber, stranger, or hired hand, the sheep desires nothing more to do with it.

What is your relationship with the Shepherd? Are you confident you know, love, and follow His voice? Do you trust His care?

_____

_____

_____

_____

What is your relationship with the opposition? Do you recognize a voice different from your Shepherd's when opposition comes toward you? Do you tend to flee from it or linger around awhile?

_____

_____

_____

_____

In the metaphor of the Shepherd and His sheep, Jesus describes Himself as personal, very close, and full of care. He calls us by name. We hear and know (recognize completely) His voice when He calls. He goes before us. We are led by Him. We follow Him to safety and to peace. He gives up His life for us to have full life. There is deep benefit to us from the Shepherd's ministry.

I hope you delight in the nearness, the familiarity, the reciprocal knowing displayed in this passage. It makes me hungry to be near God. It makes me long to be more familiar with God. I desire to recognize His voice and to follow Him when He leads me. I want to grab hold of the life He wants for me. I thirst for it again as I write about it.

How about you? Does this passage evoke desire in you?   ☐ Yes   ☐ No

The key Greek word, *GINŌSKŌ,* defined at the beginning of this lesson is the same word translated as know, in 1 John 5:20 and in John 17:3.

According to 1 John 5:20, for what reason did God come and give us understanding?

_____

_____

What is the claim made about God?

He is the _____ God and _____ .

In John 17:3, what is the claim made about knowing God?

_____

_____

In this passage, Jesus is praying to the Father for His followers. He recounts to God the purpose for why He was sent—so He could give eternal life to those under His care. Then He defines what this eternal life is. Jesus said real and eternal life is that His followers would know the one and only true God, and Jesus whom He sent. This reciprocal knowing is essential, and it has ramifications forever.

Talk to God about your thoughts and feelings from today's lesson. Share authentically with Him your reactions to Him as your Shepherd, you as His sheep, and the protection and eternal life that comes from knowing Him.

_____

_____

_____

_____

_____

_____

_____

_____

_____

_____

To Love and Be Loved - Part 1

· ·●●●·· ·

― **Key Verse** ―

Matthew 22:37-38 NIV: *"Jesus replied: 'Love the Lord your God with all your heart and with all your soul and with all your mind. This is the first and greatest commandment.'"*

· ·●●●·· ·

So far this week, we studied God's intimate presence as it relates to reciprocal seeking and knowing. I hope you are encouraged by the fervor with which God has sought you, and the depth to which He knows and cares for you moment by moment. As review, take a look at the three actions of intimacy we're focusing on this week.

Three Actions of Intimacy

1. To Seek and Be Sought
2. To Know and Be Known
3. To Love and Be Loved

Today and tomorrow, we will focus on the third of these actions.

3. To Love and Be Loved

One of my favorite stories in the Bible is that of David and his dear friend, Jonathan.

Read the following three scripture passages to hear of the affection they shared with one another.

   1 Samuel 18:1-4   **1 Samuel 20:14-17**   **2 Samuel 1:26**

Describe the relationship between these two men.

_____

_____

_____

_____

Love: ÂHAB (H157) & AHABAH (H160)

Throughout these passages, there are two Hebrew words used to describe Jonathan and David's love for each other. They are *ÂHAB* and *AHABÂH*.

ÂHAB suggests affection for and the experience of liking and/or loving. This refers to all the enjoyable, warm feelings associated with affection toward another.

AHABÂH signifies a powerful, intimate love associated with a covenant of loyalty and faithfulness.

Let's flesh this out to make the difference distinct. *Falling in love,* as culturally understood, refers to the cluster of enjoyable emotions identified in the Hebrew word, *ÂHAB.* As pleasant as *ÂHAB* is, those feelings alone fail to carry a relationship for long. We also use the word *love,* to mean something greater and deeper. In marriage, for example, we make vows (covenant) to lay down our selfish desires for the betterment of the one we love. Not only vowing to love like this, but coming through on it, is what is meant by the term *AHABÂH.*

In the context of Canadian society, covenants are made in marriage and sometimes in business, but these often lack the weight of permanence proclaimed by *AHABÂH.* Covenants created in friendship, like we are studying today, are scarce. The bond cast between David and Jonathan deviated from our cultural norm in two ways. First, it occurred between friends in innocence, and it was permanent. Please keep these differences in mind as we proceed.

> The covenant between David and Jonathan stretched far beyond their feelings. What covenants have you made in your lifetime? Were they temporary or permanent?

AHABÂH is used in 1 Samuel 18:3, 20:17 (the first-time love appears), and in 2 Samuel 1:26. *ÂHAB* is the word used in 1 Samuel 18:1 and 20:17 (the second-time love appears).

In the relationship between David and Jonathan, feelings of affection and warmth existed, as well as commitments by both men to loyalty, faithfulness, and selfless love. They shared authentic love and brimmed with rich emotion toward one another, yet the commitment established reached further than those feelings.

Do you know this kind of love? ☐ **Yes** ☐ **No**

Talk to God about your thankfulness for this kind of love, or the heartache of not knowing it. Be real with Him in whatever thoughts and feelings you have as these concepts are introduced.

_____

_____

_____

_____

_____

_____

_____

_____

Knit Together in a Covenant of Love

Read 1 Samuel 18:3 EXB below.

> *"Jonathan made an agreement [covenant; solemn pact; treaty] with David, because he loved David as much as himself [his own life, his own soul]."*

David was an impressive warrior and he caught the eye of king Saul when he killed Goliath. In meeting with Saul about this feat, David had a powerful encounter with Saul's son, Jonathan. 1 Samuel 18:1 reports the soul of Jonathan was knit together with the soul of David and resulted in a selfless love being planted in Jonathan. This tenacious love led Jonathan to make a covenant with David; one that caused him to lay down his person, his position, and his inheritance, for David's benefit.

In Israelite history, a covenant was a serious, binding, and intimate pact made between two people. Jonathan initiated such a covenant with David for only one reason: he loved him. The love Jonathan experienced for David cost Jonathan everything to which he was entitled.

I adore Jonathan. I am thrilled something was more meaningful to him than power and wealth. I cherish that his love caused him to act in a counter-cultural manner. I applaud his love—even in the form of friendship—was worth it to him. He reminds me a lot of Someone else I know. Someone who believed in covenants, love and self-sacrifice.

Read Luke 22:20 NIV.

At the Lord's supper, what did Jesus say was represented by the cup?

- The _____ _____ in His blood.

Read Matthew 26:27-28 NIV.

Again, referring to the cup, Jesus said it was, "my _____ of the

_____ which is poured out for many for the _____ of sins."

Jesus' blood served as a means of establishing covenant between God and His followers. It was poured out when He died on the cross. Jesus was motivated by the same phenomenon as Jonathan: love. That's it.

Read John 15:13 and John 3:16. What was displayed by the will of Jesus to lay down His life for the establishment of covenant?

- Great _____

There was a covenant made between Jesus and His followers. It was initiated by Jesus and based on His great love. You and I live under this deal every day. A covenant knits our soul with the Lord and is based on His love and initiation.

In this new covenant, we are given instruction.

Flip over to Matthew 22:36-38.

What does Jesus say is the imperative command in the covenant between us?

_____

Notice, just like David and Jonathan, our covenant with the Lord is based on love.

Clothed in a Royal Exchange

As we read in 1 Samuel 18:4, Jonathan gave up his robe for David. The display was deeper than two guys sharing clothes. To put on the robe of another was an outward act that represented an inner agreement to take on the identity of the other. For Jonathan to give David his robe, communicated that Jonathan gave himself up for the well-being of David. David, then, was represented by the person and position of Jonathan.

Jonathan was the rightful heir to the throne in Israel. His father was the king. King Saul hunted David for much of his reign because he wanted to protect his throne, even though David was not in pursuit of it. Surprising, but Jonathan did not possess his father's lust for power. Instead, Jonathan loved deeply. He viewed what he was entitled to as nothing in comparison to protecting his friend. Jonathan gave up his royalty and David gained it.

Don't you just esteem Jonathan? The depth of love he had for David captivates me. Now, let's consider the One with whom we have covenant.

Describe the exchanges that took place In the following verses.

Philippians 2:5-8 _____

John 13:3-7 _____

2 Corinthians 8:9 _____

Jesus exchanged the form of God for the form of man. He exchanged His position as Lord for a position of servanthood. He exchanged riches for poverty. These were not haphazard actions. He operated with purpose. Just as Jonathan gave up his position for David's gain, Jesus' exchange was for our benefit. What is the pay-off for us from Jesus' sacrifice?

2 Corinthians 8:9 _____

Galatians 3:26-27 _____

Isaiah 61:10 _____

We become rich because we are clothed with Christ's person, His salvation, and His righteousness.

When Jonathan gave up his robe and armor, he gave up himself, his position, and his inheritance. In our covenant, Jesus laid down His position as God's loved Son in heaven so we could gain our position as God's children and our inheritance in God's kingdom.

Read the following scriptures and note what we receive when we enter this covenant of love through belief in Jesus Christ.

John 1:12 _____

Ephesians 1:4-5 _____

Romans 8:17 _____

Ephesians 1:13-14 _____

Respond to the great covenant of love God made with you. Communicate with Him about the great exchange that took place for your benefit.

_____

_____

_____

_____

_____

_____

_____

_____

_____

_____

_____

_____

_____

_____

To Love and Be Loved - Part 2

Key Verse

Matthew 22:39 NIV: *"And the second is like it: 'Love your neighbor as yourself.'"*

Yesterday we probed into the relationship between David and Jonathan to get a glimpse of the love they shared. We searched scripture to learn about their hearts and the commitment of covenant to which they agreed. We also uncovered how their relationship parallels the new covenant we have with God through Jesus Christ and the associated benefits for us.

I hope you are moved by their relationship, but even more by the relationship available with the Lord. I'm cheering you on in your discovery.

Today, we delve into one more aspect of their relationship and its relevance to you and I.

Covered in Love and Grace

The pouring out of love and grace between these two men is stunning to witness. Let's explore it together.

- **Jonathan's Love and Grace for David**

If Jonathan wasn't sold out to his covenant with David, he would not have kept his promise. Jonathan had numerous temptations to renege. In fact, he was commanded to do just that.

Read 1 Samuel 20:30-31.

Why was Saul angry with Jonathan?

What did he say would never happen if David remained alive?

Saul's message was clear, "If you do not bring David to me [so I can kill him], neither you nor your kingdom will be established." To Saul's dismay, rather than cling to entitlement, Jonathan blessed David to go in safety.

Read 1 Samuel 20:41-42.

What evidence of affection is recorded in these verses?

Who gave strength to David and Jonathan's covenant?

_____

The Lord knit Jonathan and David's souls together. The Lord gave strength to the covenant between them. The Lord had great purposes to accomplish through David's kingship. The Lord had great reason to bring Jonathan alongside him. There is no friend greater than a friend so driven toward God's will she puts her own glory aside so her friend can be what the Lord calls her to be. That is a great love!

- **David's Response of Love and Grace**

We've established Jonathan's affection for David. Now it's time to examine David's fierce love for Jonathan. Remember we heard Jonathan make a request of David in 1 Samuel 20:14-17.

Read these verses again and answer the following questions.

What did Jonathan ask David to do in the future? (vs 14-15)

      a. show kindness to me & my family   b. share my coat

      c. marry my sister   d. kill my enemy

What did Jonathan ask David to do in regard to their covenant? (vs 17)

      a. reaffirm his royalty   b. reaffirm his beauty

      c. reaffirm his strength   d. reaffirm his oath

What was the basis for David's oath? (vs 17)

      a. fear   b. love   c. obligation   d. hatred

Jonathan gave up his position and his inheritance knowing David would receive it. Jonathan also asked David to honor the bond between them by showing kindness to him and his family forever—even when David rose to the powerful position that should have been Jonathan's.

Read 2 Samuel 9:1-13. Describe how David kept this covenant after Jonathan died.

_____

_____

_____

_____

_____

Years after David and Jonathan parted ways, David sought out the remaining members of Jonathan's family to show kindness to them. By this time, Jonathan and Saul were both dead. David inquired about Jonathan's family and found Mephibosheth, one of Jonathan's sons who was lame in both legs. Mephibosheth had nothing to offer David, but because of the love David had for his father, David lavished grace and blessing upon him.

In what ways did David show love to Jonathan's son in the following verses?

Verse 1: _____

Verse 5: _____

Verse 7: _____

Verse 9: _____

Verse 10: _____

There was no imminent pressure for David to fulfill his covenant with Jonathan. No repercussions would come if he backed out his oath because Saul and Jonathan were no longer alive. Still, David inquired. David initiated a search for anyone in Jonathan's household to whom he could show kindness. David desired to show his love to Jonathan, even after his death.

I can only imagine the nerves Mephibosheth felt as he approached the king. His grandfather was the preceding king who tried to destroy David. Under normal circumstances, Mephibosheth would be considered a major threat to David. Mephibosheth may have thought he was in grave danger, but as soon as David was with him, he put Mephibosheth at ease. David assured him his desire was to show kindness, not harm.

David, then, followed through. He gave Mephibosheth all the land that had belonged to king Saul and allowed Saul's servants to cultivate and harvest. Further, David insisted Mephibosheth eat at the table of the king on a regular basis. This was a great honor for Mephibosheth; a great delight for David.

Because of the bond of love between Jonathan and David, David went out of his way to love those whom Jonathan had loved. The love extended from David to Mephibosheth was the sheer delight that flows from gratitude. David loved those whom Jonathan loved because David loved Jonathan.

Read Matthew 25:34-40. Summarize the main point of this passage.

_____

_____

Yesterday we touched on Jesus' command to love the Lord with all our heart, mind, and strength.

Re-read the key verse for today to see what else Jesus asked with regard to those He loves.

In Matthew 22:39, we are told to love our _____ as ourselves.

David and Jonathan loved one another as though caring for themselves. This is precisely how we are told to love others. Jesus emphasizes that when we love those He loves—with rich affection, with commitment and loyalty, with care—we are loving Him. Love for others doesn't come from any reciprocal exchange between people. It comes from the profound gift of love from God and the gratitude-infused urge to love Him back.

When I put myself in David's shoes, I can stroll along with the choices he made. I imagine I would choose the same. But, when I take myself out of this Biblical story and look at what I choose in the present, I get stopped in my tracks.

I do have a Friend who gave up everything so I could gain a new identity, new freedom, and hope for my future. I do have a Friend who laid down everything to which He was entitled so I might be imparted His entitlements. Sometimes I fear this story is so familiar, we miss the personal application. Jesus is this Friend with whom you have a covenant of love. He is the One who paid to secure your future and your children's future.

He asks, in response, that you and I would love Him. Oh my, who wouldn't? I love Jonathan and I don't even know him. With exceeding exuberance then, I must love my Savior whom I know intimately! In response, He asks, out of this love we have for Him, we love those He loves. This is no different than Jonathan's request. Of course, David cared for Jonathan's son because of the love they shared. All the more, if you and I have been given life from Jesus, we find joy and satisfaction in loving those Jesus loves because in doing so, we love Him.

> If you have a Friend who has given extravagantly so you can have a new identity, a new freedom, and a new hope for the future, what do you desire to do in response?

I'm all jazzed up about this. I run scenarios through my mind of how I have turned away from a chance to love because it wasn't paramount to me. Then, I imagine being sick, dead or otherwise unable to care for my family and ponder how I would feel if those who said they loved me did nothing to help those I love. It'd be a tragedy. I picture how each of my kids would be distressed without me. I can't imagine those who purport to love me just idling nearby while they suffer. Ah, this is what I do to the Lord. The One who gave me everything. The Father who loves every person on earth.

How are you doing with this? Is the importance of loving others hitting home for you as it is for me? What does it mean that Jesus asks you personally to love those He loves?

_____

_____

_____

_____

1 John 4:9 states we love because Christ first loved us. Do you love? Do you accept that Christ first initiated a covenant of love with you? Talk these things out with God.

_____

_____

_____

_____

_____

_____

God loves us not because we love others, but because He has knit His heart together with yours and mine through covenant. God loves us with affection and feelings. He is not some stoic being that cannot be bothered to engage with us. He is in love with each of us. Also, He is in covenant with each of us. This covenant backs His feelings of love with a commitment to perfect faithfulness and loyalty. His is a great love given to be experienced by us.

Write out Jeremiah 31:3.

_____

_____

_____

In response to this love, gratitude drives us to love God in return. We delight in seeking, knowing, and loving Him, both with emotion and with our best covenantal love, however messy and imperfect. David and Jonathan's longing for one another caused them intense grief when their paths parted. So, it should be for us if business, or stress, or even celebration cause us to miss connection with our God.

Do you experience a depth of love for God, such that you are grieved if you miss connecting with Him? ☐ Yes ☐ No

Take a few minutes to pray about whatever thoughts and feelings are rumbling in you from the content of this lesson. Ask God to fulfill your desire for relationship with Him. Thank Him for the relationship you share with Him.

_____

_____

_____

_____

_____

_____

_____

Please remember that all the learning about God in the whole world does not negate the necessity of relating with Him. Do not be content to learn about God yet fail to interact with Him about what you are learning.

Dive Deeper 3

—··●●●··—

Search Me, O God

Read Psalm 139:1-6. Write out the verse that stands out to you the most.

_____

_____

_____

_____

Pray for Readiness to Connect with God

Example

Lord, You search me and know me. You know all my thoughts and actions. You are intimately familiar with all my ways. Thank You for knowing me. Please explore me right now and bring to my mind the truth from Your word I most need to hear. Thank You for being my Shepherd—please lead me here and now. Thank You for loving me. Help me seek You, know You, and love You back.

You can pray along with this sample prayer or write one below to better communicate your thoughts and feelings.

_____

_____

_____

_____

Listen and Confess

Be patient. Sit and wait before God. Listen to what rattles around in your mind and in your heart. Do you sense any conviction of sin, awareness of distraction, or impeding negativity? If so, confess these to God.

_____

_____

_____

_____

Review

With hindrances laid aside, ask God to lead you as you review the material from this week. Please do not skip this part, thinking you've already done the work. Learning to learn from God, to be open to His personal instruction, and to seek His voice are rich and deep blessings. I pray you will not settle for your experience of God to remain indirect, learning only through others. God will mentor you—what a thrill!

Write out the key scripture verse for each lesson this week. Then, highlight the main point you learned day by day. Make your reflections personal.

Day I: To Seek and Be Sought

Jeremiah 29:13

_____

_____

_____

Your Main Learning Point

_____

_____

_____

Day 2: To Know and Be Known

John 10:14

_____

_____

_____

Your Main Learning Point

_____

_____

_____

Day 3: To Love and Be Loved - Part I

Matthew 22:37-38

_____

_____

_____

Your Main Learning Point

_____

_____

_____

Day 4: To Love and Be Loved - Part 2

Matthew 22:39

_____

_____

_____

Your Main Learning Point

_____

_____

_____

Interact with God

To Seek and Be Sought:

- **Express to God your desire to find Him.**

_____

_____

_____

• Express to God your thoughts and feelings about His commitment to seek relationship with you.

_____

_____

_____

• Listen. Is the Holy Spirit reminding, teaching, or convicting you in some manner?

_____

_____

_____

To Know and Be Known:

• Express to God your desire to know Him more and more.

_____

_____

_____

• Express to God your thoughts and feelings about His commitment to love, approve and care for you.

_____

_____

_____

Listen. Is the Holy Spirit reminding, teaching, or convicting you in some manner?

_____

_____

_____

To Love and Be Loved:

- **Express to God your love for Him.**

_____

_____

_____

- **Express to God your thoughts and feelings about His covenant of love with you.**

_____

_____

_____

- **Express to God the reactions you have to being asked to love those He loves.**

_____

_____

_____

- **Listen. Is the Holy Spirit reminding, teaching, or convicting you in some manner?**

_____

_____

_____

Week 4

· · · ● · · ·

REVIVED

Reverence and Intimacy Collide

····•●•●•···

Head on over to www.lisadevries.ca/bigfreshfaith/
→ Watch the Video Lessons → Watch Lesson 4 and follow along below.

Two Types of Collisions:

_____ collision = billiard balls

_____ collision = train wreck

•·· The interplay between reverence and intimacy can be so complicated because as we encounter life experiences that test our faith, reverence and intimacy _____ .

Inelastic Collisions

•·· Inelastic collisions between reverence and intimacy cause _____ and

_____ .

•·· It is difficult to hold the _____ that exists within the character of God.

Elastic Collisions

•·· Elastic collisions between reverence and intimacy drive _____ and

_____ .

•·· _____ gives us our solid rock, while _____ equips us to stand on it.

•·· _____ gives us truth, while _____ equips us to live according to it.

•·· _____ comforts us when life is beyond our comprehension, while _____ allows us to abide with God in our shaky state of confusion.

•·· _____ is like our compass— _____ with the Spirit moves us in the direction it tells us to go.

Luke 17:10 NIV:

_"So you also, when you have done everything you were told to do, should say, 'We are _____ _____; we have only done our duty.'"_

Suggestions for Prayer

· Talk to God about what stirs in you from this lesson.

· Ask God for freedom from any hang ups you may have with regard to reverence and intimacy.

· Ask God to revive you with both, reverence and intimacy

· Thank God for giving both reverence and intimacy to help you find freedom in your faith.

Mercy Triumphs Over Judgment

·•● ●•·

— Key Verse —

James 2:12-13 NLT: *"So whenever you speak, or whatever you do, remember that you will be judged by the law of love, the law that set you free. For there will be no mercy for you if you have not been merciful to others. But if you have been merciful, then God's mercy toward you will win out over his judgment against you."*

·•● ●•·

Beautiful Mercy

When I reflect on the mercy of God in my life, the weight of it overwhelms me. Mercy is the most beautiful gift I have ever received. The difference in my life because of God's mercy is night and day. There are not enough words to describe its ability to revive. The life I would have, had mercy not been extended to me, is void of all I love most; the prospect is horrifying.

Mercy: ELEOS (G1656)

Mercy, as introduced by the Greek word *ELEOS,* means showing kindness toward the miserable and the afflicted with a desire to help them. It refers to having deep love that leads to compassion for those in need and showing favor to those who are loathsome.

This describes the greatest gift to me. In the midst of me being miserable, afflicted and loathsome, God shows me kindness, deep love and compassion. He desires to help me. There is nothing I've done to deserve this response. God's actions in no way match mine. There is not a day absent of reflection on this absurdity. It makes no sense, it doesn't equate, it is not a fair deal. That's the absolute treasure of God's mercy.

Read the following scriptures and match them to the phrase that highlights the importance of mercy *(ELEOS)* to our Lord.

Matthew 9:13   **The more important matters of the law are justice, mercy, and faithfulness**

Matthew 23:23   **Judgment will be merciless to the one who has shown no mercy. Mercy triumphs over judgment.**

James 3:17   **I desire mercy, not sacrifice; I came to call sinners, not the righteous**

James 2:12-13   **The wisdom that comes from heaven is full of mercy**

The Lord loves mercy! He describes it as an important matter of the law. He describes it as His desire for us and from us. He describes it as victorious.

Listen to the importance of mercy as it relates to both reverence and intimacy. Read the following verses and circle whether they connect mercy with the notion of reverence, the notion of intimacy, or both.

Ephesians 2:4-5	Reverence	Intimacy
Titus 3:4-5	Reverence	Intimacy
Psalm 5:7	Reverence	Intimacy
Habakkuk 3:2	Reverence	Intimacy
1 Peter 1:3	Reverence	Intimacy

Think back to Week 2—*The Power of Reverence*. Reverence looks straight into the heart of God and recognizes His majesty, as well as our smallness in relation. This leads to actions congruent with dependency, submission, and worship. The foundation of our faith is who God is and what He can do.

But—and there is a big but here—if all we know about God is that He is deserving of our reverence, we will miss the mark of living by faith by a long shot. Reverence gives God the credit due His name, but does not facilitate authentic relating with Him. If we only know of God's power, might and massiveness in comparison to ourselves, we would revere Him, but also steer clear of Him.

Mercy is the powerful bridge between reverence and intimacy. Mercy is the reason we can approach this great God whom we revere. Mercy is the gateway through which we crawl up into our great God's mighty arms in intimacy. Mercy is the antidote to the lie suggesting we hide from God, or try to prove ourselves to Him.

Therefore, through mercy, we are free to experience intimacy with Him. Because of mercy, we are alive in Christ even though we were dead in our transgressions. Through mercy, we are reborn and renewed by the Holy Spirit even though we are unrighteous. Through mercy, we are given living hope.

Do you see this? Without His mercy, bowing down before God in awe, would not make us alive, reborn, renewed, or given hope. What this means is without His mercy, intimacy with God would be impossible. We could not seek Him, know Him, or love Him because we would not be able to relate with Him at all.

Imagine approaching the Lord of the universe in the midst of being miserable, afflicted, loathsome—or equally absurd—prideful. Without God choosing undeserved kindness, deep love, compassion, and a desire to help you and I, all hope would be lost. The most righteous person on earth wouldn't stand a chance if God did not choose to have mercy.

Compassion

The Lord's compassion is elicited by the afflicted and the needy. He did not come to save the righteous or heal the healthy, rather, He is moved to offer compassion and mercy to those who acknowledge their need for Him to do so.

Compassion: RÂCHAM (H7355) & CHÂNAN (H2603)

To understand the compassionate heart of God, let's look also at two Hebrew words from the Old Testament. The first is *RÂCHAM,* which emphasizes deep love, tender affection, and compassion. This word is sometimes also translated, mercy. The second is *CHÂNAN,* which expresses the notion of taking pity upon, and being gracious toward.

Read the following scriptures. What actions toward God precede compassion (RÂCHAM) from God?

Psalm 103:13 _____

Proverbs 28:13 _____

Deuteronomy 30:1-3 _____

Isaiah 55:7 _____

God's mercy doesn't cost us a cent. There is nothing we can do to earn it. Nothing gives us entitlement to it. Scripture tells us; however, mercy is poured out by God to those who acknowledge their need for it. This acknowledgment is reverence in action. It nods in agreement that God is sovereign to provide mercy, and we are dependent upon Him to receive it. If I persist in rebellion and self-righteousness with no sensitivity to the Holy Spirit's conviction, I will not experience the mercy of the Lord. In this case, I will lack the reverence that equips me to call out for it. Mercy is available to me, but in order to receive it, I must acknowledge my dependency upon God for it.

My first-born was curious about the stairs in our house when he was a toddler. He wanted to learn to climb them and was angry when I put limits on his pursuit. I did not desire for him to get hurt. I tried reasoning with him and I put up obstacles to stop him, but he rebelled against my efforts. I believe in the power of natural consequences and hoped they would end these battles. Therefore, I removed the obstacles and let him explore the stairs, which he did with great emphasis on not needing help from me. All the while, my heart didn't change toward him. I still hoped for the best for him and desired to keep him safe.

He set off to climb the stairs with enthusiasm. I sat at the bottom longing to demonstrate compassion toward him. He wiggled his little body up a few, sat down and played with a toy he found. Distracted, he lost his balance and tumbled to the bottom of the stairs. I picked him up and tried to show compassion for his bruised body, but he again pushed away and climbed higher. This repeated a few times until he experienced real pain.

At that moment, my longing hadn't changed. He hadn't somehow earned my mercy, but he experienced my compassion toward him as he cried on my shoulder and acknowledged his pain. Then, he asked me to hold his hand as he climbed to the top of the stairs. In doing so, he demonstrated submission and dependence (aspects of reverence) toward me by acknowledging his need for my help. So it is with the mercy of God.

Listen to the heart of God in the following verses.

Hear His readiness and desire to share mercy with us. Remember, reconciliation is His idea. Intimacy is what He initiated with us. He does not simply tolerate the extension of mercy to us, He delights in it.

Isaiah 30:18   **Isaiah 49:15**   **Isaiah 54:10**

What do these verses tell you about the Lord's compassion toward you?

_____

_____

_____

Read Psalm 116:1-9.

Can you relate to the Psalmist?   ☐ Yes   ☐ No

Use the words of this passage to formulate your own prayer in response to God's mercy toward you.

_____

_____

_____

_____

_____

_____

_____

_____

_____

_____

_____

Cry Out for Mercy

At times, when I feel short on words to express my desire for God's mercy, I turn to the Psalms for help. In Psalm 116, God's mercy (RÂCHAM) is claimed. Now let's see how God's mercy or compassion (CHÂNAN) is outlined in the Psalms. Remember from earlier in this lesson it expresses taking pity upon and being gracious toward.

Record the various conditions of the Psalmists that prompted these pleas for compassion.

Psalm 51:1 _____

Psalm 30:10-11 _____

Psalm 31:9 _____

Psalm 6:1-2 _____

Psalm 57:1 _____

God longs to show us mercy. He turns to offer mercy to those who love Him and who call upon His name. His mercy is available to us in distress, in agony, in weakness, in sin, in disaster, and at any time of day. We can reverently cry out to the Lord, and through His mercy, He will intimately respond.

Judgment

Judgment that leads to godly discernment is helpful, but judgment that leads to condemnation of others is prohibited in scripture. Judgment of others rejects God's mercy and encourages us to become preoccupied with what others are doing. Because of the strong ties to obedience in reverence, it can be tempting to slip into condemnation of others, rather than addressing the need for intimacy with God. Judgment is an attempt to avoid one's vulnerability by casting a dark shadow on another person's shortcomings. When a person faces vulnerability and through mercy, enters into intimacy with God, he or she becomes readied to extend mercy rather than judgement to others.

Because of this, mercy is far superior to judgment. Mercy connects, judgment separates. God's plan is reconciliation. Judgment is powerless to reconcile. Mercy beats out judgment because it makes intimacy possible, even in the middle of messy, loathsome imperfection that judgment would condemn.

Mercy to Others

The Lord says in Isaiah 55:1 NIV,

> *"Come, all you who are thirsty, come to the waters; and you who have no money, come, buy and eat! Come, buy wine and milk without money and without cost."*

His mercy is free. His mercy has power to revive like that of water and food to the starving. As we receive it, God intends that we, too, would offer free mercy—that which triumphs over the judgment that separates believers. God urges us to take this seriously.

Read Luke 6:36-38. Summarize the main point of this passage.

_____

_____

Do you struggle to refrain from judging others?   ☐ Yes   ☐ No

Do you struggle to refrain from condemning others, if even in your mind?   ☐ Yes   ☐ No

Do you struggle to forgive?   ☐ Yes   ☐ No

How are you impacted by these verses that state the measure you use to show mercy, judgment, condemnation, forgiveness and generosity will be the measure used to determine the dose of each of those given to you from the Lord?

_____

_____

_____

_____

To reconcile verses in Luke 6 with those in Romans 8 is hard. One says we will be judged by what we offer while the other states there is no condemnation based on being rooted in Christ. We can be left wondering if it's safe to count on God's mercy as a free gift, or if it is conditional upon our actions toward others.

I do not believe we are asked to give what we have not received from Christ. That would be impossible because He is the creator of all things. Yet, when we have received God's intense mercy, forgiveness and generosity, which frees us from judgment and condemnation, we are held accountable for how we extend those gifts to others. Jesus explains this to us in the parable of the unmerciful servant found in Matthew 18.

Read Matthew 18:21-35.

Who was the first to forgive the debt?

_____

What did the King then expect of his servant?

_____

What is the parallel drawn to God's ways with us in verse 35?

_____

_____

Talk to God about your need for mercy and any temptation you may feel toward withholding mercy from others. You can even cry out for mercy in your struggle to be merciful. God is faithful to respond to those who call on Him with need.

_____

_____

_____

_____

_____

_____

_____

_____

_____

_____

Day 2

Grace Destroys Fear

Key Verse

2 Corinthians 12:9 NIV: *"But he said to me, 'My grace is sufficient for you, for my power is made perfect in weakness.' Therefore I will boast all the more gladly about my weaknesses, so that Christ's power may rest on me."*

Yesterday we studied mercy and the superior position it holds over judgment. We discovered mercy is integral to the integration of reverence and intimacy, and powerful to revive. I hope the Lord's intention and delight in relating with you is settling on you more and more.

Today, we are going to study the impact of grace upon reverence and intimacy. God uses grace to bring about growth in our faith, but the beautiful benefits can be hindered by fear. To become courageous in faith requires a deep soaking in mercy and grace.

The gap between reverence and intimacy is something I witness often as a therapist working toward healing, victory, and freedom in Christ. One of the harmful ramifications of separating reverence for God from intimacy with Him is the development of fear-filled faith. This can occur in two different ways.

- When people are high in reverence yet lacking intimacy, fear of mistakes and disappointing God tend to be prominent. The underlying deception hints God is superior but not trustworthy with our shortcomings. People wrought with this fear tend to be preoccupied with their performance and service to God.

- When people are high in intimacy yet lacking reverence, fear (more like an anxiety) of the unknown and hyper-vigilance tend to be struggles. The underlying deception suggests God is warm but small. People wrought with this fear tend to be preoccupied with a search for control.

Grace to Glorify God

Grace: CHARIS (G5485)

Grace, as used in our key verse today, stems from the Greek word, CHARIS. This word means the unmerited favor God exercises toward us in providing salvation. The biggest difference between the mercy we learned about yesterday, and the grace we are exploring today can be seen below.

- Mercy is to be spared the punishment our imperfection deserves
  - not getting what we do deserve

- Grace is to be given favor we have not earned
  - getting what we don't deserve

Emphasized in 2 Corinthians 12:9, God's unmerited favor was enough for Paul in his specific circumstances. In essence, the Lord told Paul that what he saw as weakness, the Lord saw as an opportunity to reveal Himself. The Lord had a plan to provide for Paul what He didn't deserve so God's power could be seen.

I get such joy from this message to Paul. What I hear is an assurance God will make something where Paul has nothing. Grace says that what the Lord can do through Paul—but also through you and I—has nothing to do with what we deserve. Instead, it has everything to do with God's power and the revelation of Himself through us.

We can be so concerned with our performance, yet I am convinced God would prefer us to be more concerned with His. God did not set out to showcase Paul. He set out to showcase Himself! He assures Paul the conditions are perfect for His plan to work, weakness and all. It was Paul who preferred less weakness and I can relate! How about you?

There are many Biblical heroes who would empathize with Paul's feelings of incompetence when God selected them to participate.

Read the following passages and match them to the list of Biblical characters who could relate to Paul. List the weaknesses they saw in themselves.

Perceived Weaknesses

Exodus 6:12	**Esther**	_____
Judges 6:13-15	**Moses**	_____
Genesis 17:16-17	**Gideon**	_____
Esther 4:11-14	**Abraham**	_____

This list could have many more. The clear point, though, is God is willing to use incompetent people to reveal Himself as competent. When God uses you or me, people may be impressed, but the million-dollar question is, "With whom will they be impressed?"

How do you feel about being used by God if it means His strength gets shown through your weakness? Would you allow others to see your weaknesses (and other ugly parts) if it meant people were impressed with the power of God displayed in you?

_____

_____

_____

_____

Destruction of Fear

Living by grace has the power to destroy fear and bring revival where life has been lost. You see, grace suggests that any positive outcomes God produces are a reflection of His power, not ours. This renders the need to perform for God—or get everything right—as silliness. Silliness, not because of the heartfelt desire in those who try to perform well for God, but silliness because of the off-track allotment of responsibility. God is not asking us for greatness. God is asking us to humbly allow Him to display His greatness in us. There is very little pressure here. It's His show, He has the starring role. People are supposed to notice Him, not us.

When our focus shifts from ourselves to God, reverence grows. If God has the power to grant unmerited favor and salvation, He must also be big enough, strong enough, majestic enough to be depended on to deliver grace. Grace builds confidence in God as the One who has the power to overcome our greatest weaknesses or difficulty.

Read 1 John 4:18.

• **According to this verse, what is the root of fear?** _____

• **What has the power to eliminate fear?** _____

Understanding why God would choose to use us is vital. It is not so we will look good or do Him a favor or avoid punishment. The prize of being used by God is being with Him in action and seeing first-hand the magnificence of Him at work. Our reverence grows from our front row seat, and our intimacy flourishes as we interact with Him in the trenches of His work.

The Discovery of Grace

In the book of Ezekiel there is a statement repeated almost 70 times, "Then they will know that I am the Lord." All through the book, God expresses His desire for His people to turn and acknowledge Him as the Lord.

To Know: YÂDA (H3045)

The verb, *to know,* in the verses of Ezekiel is a different word in the Hebrew language than we studied in our intimacy lesson. This time, the word originates from *YÂDA.* This is to learn to know, to find out and discern, to recognize or acknowledge, and to know by experience.

Highlighted by this definition, our God, who could reveal Himself in any way, chooses to invite us to participate in a life of discovering Him. Isn't that awesome? I love discovery and learning. Sadly, if we don't understand this about God, we can be so afraid of making an error in this process, we fail to risk for the sake of knowing Him more. Some of us are plagued with worry that God is not big enough to manage our imperfect efforts toward Him.

In contrast, grace communicates God's unmerited favor waiting for us when we seek Him. Hard to grasp, but God knew full well the risk He was taking in His plan to have creation free to explore Him. When I consider this, I conclude God must be willing to deal with our imperfection to gain the prize of genuine relationship.

Please do not misunderstand me here. I am not saying God is nonchalant about sin. I am not saying He fails to care whether we discern or not. I believe these things matter to

> God knew full well the risk He was taking in His plan to have creation free to explore Him. What does it mean to you that God would be willing to deal with your imperfection in order to gain genuine relationship with you?

God. What I am saying is, God has provided a way for sin and imperfection to be reconciled. He has it covered with grace!

The more plenteous problem seems to be when His people don't risk growth in their knowledge and interaction with Him. It seems God is more concerned about us participating with Him through His power and presence than about whether or not we get it right every time. Let's face it, there is no surprise for Him. We will fall short. His grace makes a way for us to embrace courage and confidence so we dare try again.

Read the following verses. What does each one teach about grace?

1 Corinthians 15:10

_____

_____

Galatians 2:21

_____

_____

2 Timothy 1:9

_____

_____

2 Corinthians 6:1

_____

_____

The grace of God has an effect. It is not meant to be cast aside for self-righteousness. He died to extend grace for free. Since the beginning of time God has had this plan. Who are we to receive His grace in vain?

What is revealed in the following scriptures about the purpose of grace?

1 Peter 4:10 _____

Ephesians 4:7 _____

Romans 12:6a _____

2 Corinthians 9:8 _____

We are to use the grace we have received to serve others. It is given to us as Christ determined, in accordance with our unique gifts. We are promised God will equip us to do every good work He asks of us.

Read Philippians 4:6-7. What indicates that grace destroys fear?

_____

_____

God's grace allows us to pray and feel peace even in the midst of scary circumstances. It allows our hearts and minds to be protected. God's grace destroys fear, thus making intimacy with God possible, and fresh faith a reality.

Take time to process your thoughts and feelings about this lesson with God. If you struggle with fear, wrestle with God about how He intends His grace to bring freedom to you. Reflect on God's grace to you.

_____

_____

_____

_____

_____

_____

_____

_____

_____

_____

Unity Quiets Dissension

Key Verse

John 17:23 NLT: *"I am in them and you are in me. May they experience such perfect unity that the world will know that you sent me and that you love them as much as you love me."*

So far this week, we've explored how reverence and intimacy fuel freedom in faith. We saw mercy and grace as bridges between God's holiness and our imperfection, while judgment and fear separate.

Today, we will discuss unity and dissension.

Before we get started, let's approach the Lord together.

Lord, we need You. You are a God who cherishes unity, but it is hard. I pray You use Your mighty power to break down walls of dissension that may or may not be detected by us at this time. God, we want to live according to Your instructions. Your ways are the best for us. Please help us surrender anything that could tie us to dissension, rather than unity. Please give us courage to obey You. By Your name and power, Jesus, amen.

Unity: HEIS (G1520)

To be united is to be bound together. Unity refers to a bond and implies agreement. In our key verse today, the word translated as, *unity,* is *HEIS,* and means to be one.

Read John 17:20-23.

Jesus prayed for His disciples in the verses proceeding these. We pick up here as He prays for all who believe in Him as a result of the message the disciples are about to spread.

Jesus longs for two things for all those who believe in Him. What are they? (vs 21)

1. _____

2. _____

What does Jesus tell believers to use as a model for their unity? (vs 22)

_____

Jesus explains the links of unity like this:

Unity between Jesus and the Father

Unity between believers and the Father, Spirit, and Son

Unity between Believers

What will the world know as a result of this unity? (vs 21 and 23)

_____

_____

_____

Read the following verses.

John 16:12-15   John 14:16-17

What evidence shows the Holy Spirit shares unity with the Father and the Son?

_____

What evidence shows the Holy Spirit shares unity with believers?

_____

Jesus talked to His Father (with whom He is united) about the benefits of unity. He expressed desire for those who follow Him to grasp its beauty and power, then display a similar, impressive togetherness to the world. Intimacy is required to form such deep bonds, but to be maintained, reverence must secure it to a foundation of truth.

Think for a moment about those with whom you feel the most unified. These could be individuals you know or people groups you know about. What is the bond?

_____

_____

_____

_____

_____

_____

_____

_____

Think for a moment about those with whom you feel the least unified. Again, think about those you know and those who represent a perspective. What is at the root of the disagreement or disunity you experience with them?

_____

_____

_____

_____

_____

Dissension

Dissension refers to a disagreement that leads to discord, tension or strife. In Galatians 5:19-20, discord and dissension are listed as acts of the flesh, which are to be avoided.

Listen to the descriptions of dissension and division present in the following verses.

1 Timothy 6:3-5   Titus 3:10-11

What do these verses tell us about those who stir up dissension?

_____

_____

Harsh words, right? Consider not who we may judge as being guilty of this, but rather how we may participate in this. Dissension destroys unity and damages the goal Jesus expressed in our key verse. Jesus has great plans for our unity. He intends it as a display of His character, His identity and His love. Because dissension hinders unity, we ought to guard against being the instigator of it!

Stop here and ask God to examine your heart. Ask Him if you are guilty of stirring up dissension or disunity. If conviction rises, stop and confess your sin to God. Ask God to forgive you and show you how to move forward in unity.

_____

_____

_____

_____

_____

If you have been hurt by dissension and disunity, pray. Share your thoughts and feelings with God. Ask Him to heal to your wounds.

_____

_____

_____

_____

_____

_____

One

Ephesians 4 NIV, emphasizes the importance of unity among believers.

Read Ephesians 4:1-4. Check all the descriptors used for how we ought to live with faith.

_____In solitude   _____In humility   _____In fear   _____In love   _____In patience

_____In gentleness   _____In arrogance   _____In peace   _____In self-righteousness

Fill in the blanks below from verse 4-6.

"There is _____ body and _____ Spirit, just as you were called to _____ hope when you were called; _____ Lord, _____ faith, _____ baptism; _____ God and Father of all, who is over all and through all and in all."

Now jump to Ephesians 4:11-16.

What was God's purpose in giving some people as apostles, prophets, evangelists, pastors and teachers? (vs 12)

_____

What is His goal in building up the body of Christ? (vs 13)

_____

When this is accomplished, what will we be guarded against? (vs 14)

_____

What will allow us to grow into the mature body of Christ? (vs 15)

_____

Fill in the blanks from verse 16 below.

"From [Christ] the whole body, joined and held together by every supporting ligament, grows and builds itself up in _____ , as _____ _____ does its work."

Unity is an antidote to dissension. As the body of believers walk in God's power and presence, they display humility, patience, gentleness, love, and peace. With this reflection of Him in us, we become unified—one in hope, faith, and baptism. We also become unified in one Spirit, one Lord Jesus, and one Father of all. God provides for His body to become mature, protected against dissension and working together in love.

We are not all in the same place along this road. We do not have the same strengths and weaknesses. We have not been taught via the same experiences. We must protect Christ's body against the dissension that rises up from acceptable differences. When we do not, we labor against the goal of Christ being glorified here on earth.

Read 1 Corinthians 12:12-27. This passage may be familiar to many of you. Consider this perspective: How could your acceptance of the diversity of the body help you avoid dissension?

_____

_____

_____

How can understanding the function of the body of Christ help you grow to maturity?

_____

_____

_____

Unity is a picture of intimacy at work—intimacy with God and intimacy with others—causing oneness to be experienced. But this oneness flourishes where reverence for God is shared. God instructs us to be unified *in Him*. This implies both the reverence to acknowledge who God is and who we are in comparison, and the intimacy to think and behave as one.

To say we agree about who God is, then live with dissension between us makes no sense. On the other hand, when we reject what God asks of us for the purpose of avoiding conflict, we become fools. When the church dismisses the authority of God or devours one another because of it, tragedy happens. Reverence and intimacy morph into a breeding ground for dissension and, in turn, birth destruction.

On the flip side, when the power of reverence and intimacy causes believers to experience unity with God and with others, miracles happen. People of faith become persuaded by the truth about God, they stand unified in their trust of Him, and they share expectation He will come through as Lord in their community. In this case, faith thrives not just within individuals, but in relationships and churches too.

Express to God your desire for unity with the Holy Spirit, Jesus, and Himself. Ask Him to equip you and support you in pursuing unity with other believers (including the difficult ones).

_____

_____

_____

_____

_____

Confidence Frees From Legalism

2 Corinthians 3:5 NIV: *"Not that we are competent in ourselves to claim anything for ourselves, but our competence comes from God."*

Driving Perfection

In my first few years as a follower of Christ (in my early 20's), I felt confused by legalism. I desired to obey God but didn't want to be trapped by unnecessary rule-keeping. I heard believers proclaim, "Obedience expresses love toward God," but I also observed those who wanted to justify dishonesty or indulgence say, "Well, there is no need to be legalistic."

In response to this, I embarked on an experiment. I figured if I could live according to every rule for some period of time, I would gain insight into the benefits and harm of legalism. I knew all around perfection was out of the question, so I compromised. I set out to obey every law written about how to drive a car for a full week.

As my experiment started, my hands were at ten and two, my eyes on high alert, and my feet at the ready to come to complete stops and submit to all speed limits. With a little practice, I improved. I observed with heightened attention. I resisted the urge to speed. I stopped before the white lines at every intersection. I ensured the right person went first at all four way stops. With precision, I shoulder checked, signaled, and never left my high beams on to blind oncoming drivers.

Within a couple days, I could get from my home to town and back without a single mistake. I attained superstar driver status in my mind. Good for me, right?

You know what two things I also became excellent at? First, I became great at focusing on myself. Second, I became great at finding fault in other drivers. I realized there are too many haphazard drivers out there who don't follow the rules of the road. I could pick out errors everywhere I went. I compared my precision with their lackluster performances and became convinced I was superior behind the wheel.

I was astounded at the rapid onslaught of new thoughts. Legalism is a powerful, mind-altering condition. Before this endeavor, driving was just a means to an end. I was mindful of safety, but didn't get my knickers in a knot over traffic violators. I paid little attention to my performance the majority of the time. Within a few short days, I was arrogant over my success and judgmental of other's mistakes. I was motivated to do everything "right", rather than embrace to the larger concept of safety.

> Legalism is a powerful, mind-altering condition which breeds arrogance and judgement. Can you think of a time when you have experienced its lure?

The legalism spoken of in Christian circles refers to the belief that adherence to certain rules or laws have the power to attain or maintain salvation.

Imagine if I believed my success at driving earned me (or dictated the nature of) eternal life. If this were true, driving well would set me up for arrogance and judgment, whereas driving errors would elicit self-depreciation and envy. Either way, if my performance dictated the eternal outcome, I would be consumed with myself, how I compared to others, and the specific rules rather than the big picture application of the rules. This is the tragedy of legalism.

Jesus highlights the error of legalism in Luke 14:1-6. Read this passage and answer the questions below.

Jesus kept His Father's commands (John 15:10), yet the Pharisees believed He was guilty of violating one. Which one?

_____

What was the big picture motivation overlooked by the Pharisees in their judgment of Jesus?

_____

God intends for us to understand His heart. He desires our comprehension of His purposes not only His instructions. Imagine a parent who has taught her child not to cross the street alone. The rule is, don't cross the street. The goal of the rule is to keep the child safe. Now imagine a big house is on fire and the flames are encroaching on the child while she stands on the sidewalk without her parent. Legalism suggests obedience is to stay put and get burned. Understanding the heart of the matter makes it clear in this circumstance it is wise to avoid death by moving across the street.

I am convinced legalism robs us. It interrupts the beautiful interplay intended by God for reverence and intimacy by shifting our focus to ourselves. Legalism discounts what God has done for us and eggs us to obsess over what we ought to do for God. The motivation not being the intimate love we share with Him, but instead a preoccupation with covering our butt before Him.

Legalism is such a powerful distraction to what God would otherwise accomplish. It firmly fixes our focus on our own performance, and leads us to judge others accordingly. Legalism nullifies the effectiveness of God's grace, mercy, and plan for unity.

Confidence in Christ

Read our key verse, 2 Corinthians 3:5.

How does this proclamation differ from the conclusions that stem out of legalism?

_____

_____

Confidence in Christ is different from the preoccupation with self, produced by legalism.

Read the following scriptures and note the statements that reflect confidence in Christ rather than in the flesh.

Philippians 4:13

_____

_____

John 15:5

_____

_____

1 Corinthians 2:1-5

_____

_____

Philippians 1:6

_____

_____

1 John 2:28

_____

_____

2 Corinthians 5:17

_____

_____

When faith is tested, God's intention is purification and growth. Every time we step out to trust God with something new, or something old for the hundredth time, an opportunity for God to grow fresh faith in us exists. As we have already studied, faith is perfected as our circumstances force reverence for God and intimacy with God to meet one another. Anytime we are willing to turn the situations challenging our faith over to God, we benefit from what He reveals. The Lord delights to prove Himself to us and to prove what He is able and willing to do through us. This builds confidence, not in our abilities, but in His.

We need to guard ourselves from becoming distracted by our abilities (or lack thereof), and with the shortcomings (or daunting successes) of others. When we fail to do this, it stunts the reviving power of reverence and intimacy; and therefore, faith.

Do you tend to get caught up in legalism, or gain confidence in Christ? Do you tend to evaluate what you can and can't do, or what God can do through you?

_____

_____

_____

_____

_____

If you are sitting with conviction over legalism, confess it to God and thank Him for forgiveness.

_____

_____

_____

_____

_____

When sin or error is exposed, people are set free. God does not convict in order to condemn. Rather, He convicts in order to set us free. Trust God's grace and mercy to cover both your participation in legalism and any accusations about your character being hurled at you because of it. Healing and freedom sometimes require surgery. Thankfully, we have a top-notch surgeon.

Read Philippians 3:3-14 NIV.

What were Paul's reasons for having confidence in his flesh? (vs 4-6)

_____

_____

For whose sake did Paul lose all of these things? (vs 8)

_____

He traded a righteousness of his own for the _____ **that comes from**

_____ **on the basis of** _____ **. (vs 9)**

What does Paul focus on in order to press forward in his life of faith? (vs 13-14)

_____

_____

Paul (when he was known as Saul) was at the top of the class when it came to legalism. He was dialed in for success and superiority, but when he encountered Christ, his sources of pride became like garbage in comparison to knowing Christ. Christ became his entire focus. His confidence shifted from his flesh to Christ. This is the transformation God desires for each of us as the parameters of our faith are expanded.

Ask God to reveal to you what you have confidence in. If you struggle to have confidence and instead are plagued with insecurity, ask Him to reveal to you the reason that confidence in Christ escapes you. Take time to wait and listen for this insight.

_____

_____

_____

_____

_____

_____

If you so desire, ask God to bring experiences into your life to teach you to place your confidence in Him alone.

_____

_____

_____

_____

Talk to God about your thoughts and feelings about legalism, and building confidence in Christ. If any part of this lesson is difficult, take time to wrestle it out with the Lord.

_____

_____

_____

_____

_____

Dive Deeper 4

— ··•◦●◦•·· —

Wash Me, O God

Write out Psalm 51:10-12.

_____

_____

_____

_____

_____

Pray for Readiness to Connect with God

┌─── *Example* ──────────────────────────────┐

My Lord, please create a pure heart in me, renew my spirit. Remain united with me as You promise. Please fill me with joy based on Your mercy, Your grace, Your unity, and the confidence I have in You. Make my spirit willing to lay down judgment, fear, dissension, and legalism, so I may grow in reverence and intimacy with You. Please build my faith on Your solid foundation, so it will be sustained by Your power and presence.

└──┘

You can pray along with this sample prayer or write one below to better communicate your thoughts and feelings.

_____

_____

_____

_____

_____

_____

Listen and Confess

Be patient. Sit and wait before God. Listen to what rattles around in your mind and in your heart. Do you sense any conviction of sin, awareness of distraction, or impeding negativity? If so, confess these to God.

_____

_____

_____

_____

_____

_____

Review

With hindrances laid aside, ask God to lead you as you review the material from this week. Please do not skip this part, thinking you've already done the work. Learning to learn from God, to be open to His personal instruction, and to seek His voice are rich and deep blessings. I pray you will not settle for your experience of God to remain indirect, learning only through others. God will mentor you—what a thrill!

Write out the key scripture verse for each lesson this week. Then, highlight the main point you learned day by day. Make your reflections personal.

Day I: Mercy Triumphs Over Judgment

James 2:12-13

_____

_____

_____

Your Main Learning Point

_____

_____

_____

Day 2: Grace Destroys Fear

2 Corinthians 12:9

_____

_____

_____

Your Main Learning Point

_____

_____

_____

Day 3: Unity Quiets Dissension

John 17:23

_____

_____

_____

Your Main Learning Point

_____

_____

_____

Day 4: Confidence Frees from Legalism

2 Corinthians 3:5

_____

_____

_____

Your Main Learning Point

_____

_____

_____

Study Skills

My understanding of scripture is enhanced by word studies. They are present in many homework lessons throughout this book. To study words often causes me surprise and delight as I discover rich details about the author's intent.

There are resources available online to expand your Bible study skills and journey deeper into God Word without being dependent upon someone else to explore for you.

Go to www.blueletterbible.org.

Type the key verse from day one this week, James 2:12-13, in the search bar. Select either the KJV or the NASB from the drop-down menu of Bible versions below the search bar. Press the search key.

When the verses appear on your screen, look along the navigation menu at the top of the page to find the word, "Strong's". Click the box beside it to make Strong's numbers appear beside the text. These numbers allow you to look up the indicated word in the original language and explore its definition.

The focus of the day one lesson was mercy. Click on the number beside the word *mercy* to see more information. Here you can learn about the original Greek word, view dictionary entries, and probe the usage of *mercy* within the Bible. At the bottom of the page, you can access a concordance which outlines other appearances of the word throughout scripture. This provides more context for the operation of the word.

Select two key verses from your study this week and write the references below. Next to each one, specify a word contained in the verse that you desire to explore further.

Verse Reference	Word of Interest
1. _____	_____
2. _____	_____

Proceed to blueletterbible.org and enter your verse reference. When the scripture appears, select "Strong's" and click on the number beside your chosen word of interest. Explore the information provided and record facts of interest, insight or further questions.

1. _____

_____

_____

_____

2. _____

_____

_____

_____

Interact with God

Pray about what you learned. Incorporate the new discoveries into your conversation with God. Share your thoughts and feelings with Him. Thank Him for what He has imparted to you this week.

_____

_____

_____

_____

_____

_____

_____

_____

A FRESH LOOK AT THE AGE-OLD DESIGN

The Consistency of God

··•●•··

Head on over to www.lisadevries.ca/bigfreshfaith/
→ **Watch the Video Lessons** → **Watch Lesson 5 and follow along below.**

●·· The Bible tells the story of one plan, made by one God, being fulfilled with _____ .

Matthew 5:17 NIV:

"Do not think that I've come to abolish the law or the prophets. I have not come to abolish them but to _____ them."

●·· God's _____ of reverence and intimacy can be seen in the Trinity, in heaven, in the tabernacle and temple, in Christ, and in us.

The Design of the Trinity

●·· Reverence and intimacy were not given only as tools to help us. They are qualities that exist in the design of _____ , Himself.

The Design of God's Throne in Heaven

· **The Vault:** A great expanse, sparkling like _____ ; signifying God's infinite and sweeping _____ ;

· **The Throne:** Made of brilliant shades of blue like lapis lazuli—a stone representing _____ , honor, _____ and trust.

· **The Figure:** A man glowing like hot metal and full of _____ .

· **The Voice:** John pointed out his _____ with the voice; it had spoken to him before.

· **The Rainbow:**
  · A sign of a _____ God made with man and all living creatures; and
  · It serves as a reminder to God to _____ destroy us for our wickedness.

●·· We lock in a sense of _____ and _____ that He is trustworthy and full of integrity from the moment of earth's inception to the end of eternity!

Suggestions for Prayer

· Talk to God about what stirs in you from this lesson.

· Reflect on the imagery in these passages of scripture. Worship God for His grandeur.

· Consider God's unwillingness to destroy you because of your sin. Ask Him to help you have the courage and confidence to approach Him through His mercy.

· Thank God for His greatness and His mercy.

The Mercy Seat - Part 1

> ### Key Verse
>
> Exodus 25:22a NKJV: *"And there I will meet with you, and I will speak with you from above the mercy seat..."*

I hope the truths presented this week impact you on a personal level and draw you into greater faith. I pray you are empowered by reverence and intimacy to move toward freedom and victory even if life is coming at you with relentlessness.

From the introductory lesson for Week 5, the picture of God's throne brings words to my mind like majesty, glory, exuberance, luxury, and power. I glimpse His greatness and am filled with reverence. I fear such a powerful God. I know I am nothing, and have no defense to whatever He wills for me. He is sovereign. I am clearly not.

Then, full of wonder, I contemplate His promise never to destroy me because of my sinfulness, and His mercy washes over me. My reverence does not isolate me from God, rather because of His mercy, it draws me to Him in intimacy. My smallness in comparison to Him does not make me hide in shame, it makes me run to Him as my refuge and my strength. God's throne in heaven anchors my faith in both reverence and intimacy.

I wish we could sit and discuss these points of learning. I would love to know how you are integrating this knowledge with the events of your life. I'm curious about your interaction with God and what He illuminates for you. I know He is at work. I am cheering for His will and your victory.

God's Earthly Throne

This week we are set to study the earthly throne of God as it appeared during the times of the Old Testament and the New Testament. The Lord is consistent. He does not change. He is the everlasting God.

Let's start by checking out God's throne within the tabernacle in a two-part lesson. We will focus on the days of Moses and the Israelites while they were camped in the wilderness near Mount Sinai. At this time in history, Moses was leading the Israelites from Egypt, where they had been enslaved for the past 400 years, to the land of Canaan, which had been promised to Abraham many generations before. Jump with me into this story from Exodus 24. It occurs at a time when Moses was called by God to go up to Mount Sinai to be in the presence of the Lord.

Read Exodus 24:15-18 NIV and fill in the blanks below.

When Moses went up on the mountain, the _____ (that represented God's presence) covered it. Moses stayed on the mountain with God for _____ days and nights, engulfed in the glory of the Lord.

While Moses was on the mountain, God confided in him. He gave him instructions regarding the tabernacle (Exodus 25-31), and gave him the ten commandments on two stone tablets (Exodus 31:18). Today we will focus on part of the instructions for the tabernacle and the location of the ten commandments within it. These two items are greatly intertwined, as you will discover.

Read Exodus 25:10-22 to hear the instructions God gave to Moses about how to build the Ark of the Covenant and the Mercy Seat (also called the Atonement Cover).

The Ark of the Covenant

The Ark was to be made of _____ wood. (vs.10) It was to be _____ cubits long, _____ cubits wide, and _____ cubits high. (vs.10) It was to be overlaid with _____ . (vs.11)

Read Exodus 25:16.

"Then put in the ark the tablets of the _____ law, which I will give you."

This covenant was spoken by God to Moses in Exodus 20 and is known as the ten commandments. At the conclusion of Moses' time with God on Mount Sinai, God gave this testimony to him written on tablets of stone by the very finger of God (Ex. 31:18 NLT).

The Mercy Seat

Now let's learn about the Mercy Seat.

Read Exodus 25:17-22 NIV.

The atonement cover was also to be made of _____ . (vs.17) It was also to be _____ cubits long, and _____ cubits wide (vs.17)—the exact measurements of the Ark of the Covenant.

In addition, it was to have a _____ made of _____ at either end of the Mercy Seat. (vs.19) These two cherubim were to be made out of _____ gold. (vs.18) The cherubim were to have their _____ spread upward, overshadowing the cover with them. (vs 20) They were to be positioned across from each other, with their faces turned toward the _____ . (v.20)

So far, we know there was to be a box made with acacia wood and overlaid with pure gold inside and out, and gold moldings around it. This was called the Ark of the Covenant. Inside the Ark, the stone tablets containing the ten commandments were placed.

There was to be made a Mercy Seat (or Atonement Cover) of pure gold with the exact dimensions of the Ark. Two cherubim were put upon it, positioned at either end so they were facing the Mercy Seat between them, with wings raised upward and covering the Mercy Seat.

The Mercy Seat was to be put on _____ of the Ark and the tablets of the covenant law were to be put _____ . (vs.21)

Read verse 22, in its entirety, from the NASB below.

> *"There I will meet with you; and from above the Mercy Seat, from between the two cherubim which are upon the ark of the testimony, I will speak to you about all that I will give you in commandment for the sons of Israel."*

In summary, the Mercy Seat or Atonement Cover sat on top of the Ark that contained the ten commandments, and it was from there God met with His people and instructed them.

Sketch a picture of this below. Draw an uncovered box to represent the Ark of the Covenant. Inside the box, place the two stone tablets. On top of the box, draw a lid with a cherub on either end. And above the lid (between the cherubim), draw a cloud to represent the presence of the Lord.

The Mercy Seat

Mercy Seat: KAPPÔRETH (H3727)

To fully understand the significance of the Mercy Seat, let's examine what this term means. In Exodus 25, the term, *Mercy Seat,* is translated from the Hebrew word *KAPPÔRETH. KAPPÔRETH* is a noun which means a lid or cover. The Mercy Seat is, therefore, a lid or cover that rests on top of the Ark of the Covenant.

One of the most beautiful aspects of the Mercy Seat can be seen in the associated root word, *KÂPHAR* (H3722). *KÂPHAR* also means to cover, but it is used in a different sense. *KÂPHAR* is associated with covering over or purging. It means to cover in such a way as to make an atonement, make reconciliation, or cover over. Therefore, the Mercy Seat was to sit as a lid on top of the Ark—not simply a regular lid—but a covering representing a means of making atonement or reconciliation.

We see again and again the interplay between majesty and mercy. In this part of the tabernacle, there was gold, precious wood, elaborate design—all things intended to reflect God's greatness, and there was the Mercy Seat—intended to communicate God's invitation and provision for us to experience intimacy with Him.

God's Plan of Mercy

Let's continue on to put this together with what God told Moses to place in the Ark. God's instructions were for Moses to put the stone tablets which contained the ten commandments into the Ark. The ten commandments represent the conditions of the old covenant between the Israelites and God.

Turn to God's words in Exodus 19:5-6 NIV to highlight this covenant.

God informed Moses to tell the Israelites the conditions of His covenant with them. The Israelites were given the responsibility to _____ God's instructions and keep His _____ . (vs 5) In exchange, God promised the Israelites that they would be a kingdom of _____ and a _____ nation. (vs 6)

The ten commandments written on the stone tablets were like the rule book the Israelites were to follow in order to be God's special possession in this world. They were to obey these rules and, in exchange, God would hold them up as a holy nation. Both the Israelites and God had responsibility in this covenant.

Think through this with me. In the same meeting between God and Moses, God wrote out these rules for the Israelites, then instructed Moses to place them inside the Ark of the Covenant and cover them with a lid of mercy. At the precise time God gave the Israelites the law, He positioned mercy on top of it. God gave His people instructions to follow out of reverence, and through His provisions for their inability to succeed, He made intimacy possible.

Let that sink in for a minute. He gave them the law and covered their inability to keep it, with mercy. Do you hear the consistency of our Lord? From the deliverance of the rules His people were to obey, God planned deliverance from the punishment their disobedience ought to bring. From the inception of the law, God has been covering the law with mercy. As believers in Jesus Christ, we worship a God who has been full of mercy through all time.

This truth brings tears to my eyes and fills my heart with gratitude. Oh Lord, where would I be without Your great merciful heart toward Your people? I hope this soaks in like water to a sponge.

How does God's mercy, displayed in this aspect of the tabernacle design, impact your thoughts and feelings about approaching Him?

_____

_____

_____

_____

Talk to God about Your thoughts and feelings toward His character of mercy.

_____

_____

_____

_____

The Mercy Seat - Part 2

— ••●•• —

Yesterday we looked at the tabernacle design of the Ark of the Covenant and the Mercy Seat. I hope you were encouraged by God's intention to position mercy on top of the law, right from the moment the law was given. Our God spurs on our faith as He reveals His character and actions through time.

God's Purpose for Mercy

We will continue on with our key verse from yesterday as there is more to unpack. Take a moment to read it again. Now let's back up a bit and start our lesson today with the first 8 verses of Exodus 25.

Read Exodus 25:1-8.

In verses 1 through 7, God told Moses to take up a free will offering for all the materials needed to build the tabernacle. In verse 8, God stated the purpose for His plan.

What was God's purpose in asking Moses to oversee the building of a sanctuary for Himself?

_____

God desired a place to be with His people in a tangible way. He desired to dwell with them, to meet with them, to commune with them. It was the place God planned to live among His people. It's significant to me that God would want to do such a thing. What a great God we worship!

Exodus 25:2-7 highlights the materials God told the Israelites to use to build His house. List those materials.

_____

_____

_____

_____

Let's take a look at some of the ways these materials were to be used in the Lord's place of dwelling. We will not do an exhaustive study of the tabernacle design here, rather study a snapshot of how these materials were put to use. To read the full directions given regarding the tabernacle, you could read all of chapters 25-30, but for our study today, I will highlight a few key verses.

Read the Exodus passages and note the materials used to build the corresponding articles.

	Article Made	Materials used
Exodus 25:23-24	Table of showbread	_____
Exodus 25:31	Lampstand	_____
Exodus 26:1	Curtains	_____
Exodus 26:31-32	Veil	_____
Exodus 27:1-2	Altar	_____
Exodus 28:2-6	Priests' garments	_____
Exodus 30:1-5	Altar of incense	_____
Exodus 30:23-25	Anointing oil	_____
Exodus 30:34-35	Incense	_____

What is your impression of this building?

_____

_____

It strikes me this is no meagre dwelling. In fact, it sounds like no home I've visited. Who would live in such an elaborate place?

Read the following verses and record the position of God revealed.

God's Position

Psalm 145:1	_____
Psalm 47:2, 7	_____
Psalm 95:3	_____

Our God is a King, and it seems fitting that when He gave instructions about where He would reside to be among His people, He described an elaborate palace—a place made with gold, silver, and bronze, strong wood, and luxurious linens.

Focus on Exodus 25:2. Where were the Israelites supposed to get the materials to build such an amazing palace for their King?

_____

_____

Moved: NÂDAB (H5068)

God instructed the Israelites to give as their hearts were moved. This word, *moved,* comes from the Hebrew word *NÂDAB.* This word is used to describe the free, voluntary desire of the heart to give oneself or of one's resources to the service of the Lord. God's palace was to be built with great riches that flowed from eager hearts, motivated to give to the Lord.

Read Exodus 36:2-7. Describe the manner in which the Israelites gave to the Lord.

_____

God enlisted all those whose hearts were willing to give (vs 2), then inspired all those who He had endowed with special skills (vs 2) to construct an intricately designed palace for Himself (chapters 25-30) so He could be with His people. I love this King!

Now, with all this talk about our King and His majestic palace, let's find out about His throne.

Read 2 Samuel 6:2.

In this passage, David brings the Ark of the Covenant back to the Israelites after a time when it had been stolen. Look at the word used to describe how God sits between the cherubim. God is _____ between the cherubim.

Also, consider the words in Isaiah 37:16 and Psalm 99:1. Where is the Lord positioned?

_____

A throne between the cherubim is a reference to the two cherubim at the ends of the Mercy Seat or Atonement Cover. From this, we can conclude the Mercy Seat is not only a significant blessing to God's people, but it is also the supreme throne of God among His people.

We reflected yesterday on the beauty of God's character shown through the Mercy Seat as it was placed over the law. Today, it is fitting to acknowledge that the throne of the Lord matches His character. Earthly kings build their thrones out of their great riches, our King is no different.

In what ways is our King rich?

Isaiah 63:7 _____

Psalm 145:8 _____

Ephesians 2:4 _____

Psalm 86:5, 15 _____

Let the significance of this percolate. God instructs His people and provides for their shortcomings at the same time. Kings build their thrones out of their riches. Our God, who is the King of all kings, chose for Himself a throne made rich in love, kindness, grace, and mercy—a throne purposed for atonement and reconciliation. This is a most mighty, unusual, and praiseworthy King!

God sits enthroned in Heaven full of majesty. A glimpse of Him on His throne causes humans and heavenly creatures to fall on their faces before Him. In the days of the tabernacle, God sat enthroned on earth in similar greatness and beauty. His palace was made of the finest materials our world has to offer. God is worthy of respect and awe, and the Israelites delighted in offering their skills and wealth to Him.

What is your response to the design of God's earthly throne?

_____

_____

_____

_____

Talk with God about what you learned today. Build into the relationship you can have with this awesome God.

_____

_____

_____

_____

_____

_____

_____

Day 3

The Sacrifice of Atonement - Part 1

······●··

Key Verse

Romans 3:25a NIV: : *"God presented Christ as a sacrifice of atonement, through the shedding of his blood—to be received by faith."*

Over the past two days of study we examined truths about God's throne within the tabernacle and the implications for us. I hope you are experiencing God's mercy and intimacy in the midst of His reverential position upon His throne. Remember, knowledge about God is all for naught, if not to impact our relationship with Him.

Ask God to reveal Himself more to you today. Express to Him your longing to know Him more, not just to know more stuff about Him.

_____

_____

Today we will look into the function of the Mercy Seat, then we will springboard into the New Testament.

Read the following verses.

    1. Leviticus 16:1-2 NIV

What was the consequence Aaron's two sons experienced after approaching the presence of the Lord? (vs 1)

_____

Aaron also was told he would experience a consequence if he entered the holy place of the tabernacle. Unless he prepared according to God's instructions, death was imminent if he went beyond the veil into the holy place that contained the Ark of the Covenant, the Mercy Seat, and the presence of the Lord.

    2. Leviticus 16:3-5

In order to enter the Lord's presence, Aaron was instructed to offer two things as sin offerings. What were they?

A _____ **(vs 3) and two** _____ **(vs 5).**

    3. Leviticus 16:11-14

What was the purpose of the bull offering? (vs 11)

_____

Aaron was given specific instructions to:

- Bring coals from the atonement sacrifice and two handfuls of incense inside

  the _____ . (vs 12)

- Put the incense on the fire before the Lord so a cloud of incense covered

  the _____ . (vs 13)

- Take some of the _____ of the bull and sprinkle it on

  the _____ seven times. (vs 14)

  4. Leviticus 16:15

What was the purpose of the goat offering?

_____

What was to be done with the blood from the goat?

_____

These actions (as well as some others), were designed to purify the Most Holy Place beyond the veil where the Ark, the Mercy Seat, and the presence of the Lord resided. Verse 16 tells us this was needed because of the impurities of the people of Israel and because of their transgressions and sins.

  5. Leviticus 16:20-22

What was different about the goat used in these verses? (vs 20)

_____

What was to be put on the goat? (vs 21)

_____

What was the goat to do next? (vs 22)

_____

In these verses God made a way for Aaron to approach His presence. This was made possible by atonement blood, sprinkled on the Mercy Seat, and by the sins of Israel being put upon a scapegoat who carried them away to a remote place. This atonement was to occur every year for the sins of the Israelites.

The Mercy Seat

Mercy Seat: HILASTĒRION (G2435)

In the New Testament, the Greek word, *HILASTĒRION*, appears twice, and is translated as, *Mercy Seat* or *Atonement Cover*. It points to an atoning victim, and references the lid of the Ark of the Covenant. *HILASTĒRION* means to make propitiation. Propitiation is an action meant to regain someone's favor or make up for something done wrong. So, when this word is used in the New Testament, it refers to the Mercy Seat and the atonement that happens upon it.

Read Hebrews 9:1-15. What a rich passage! Try to put the main points of this passage in your words.

_____

_____

_____

_____

_____

If you were a Jewish person living at the time this passage was written, how would these truths change your life?

_____

_____

_____

In the days of the tabernacle, the high priest offered the blood of animals and followed regulations to enter the Most Holy Place. These sacrifices were never complete and were redone every year. When Christ came, died, and was resurrected to a more perfect tabernacle in heaven, His blood allowed Him to enter the Most Holy Place and secure payment for the sins of all people forever. Because of Jesus' blood upon the Mercy Seat, we are forever purified from sin and set free to approach the living God in intimacy.

To hear the second New Testament reference to the Mercy Seat, read Romans 3:21-26. Hone in on our key scripture verse for the day, verse 25 NIV, and fill in the blanks below.

"God presented _____ as a _____ of _____ ,
through the shedding of His _____ —to be received by _____ ."

These verses explain that the requirements of the law got trumped by the righteousness of God being passed to believers through faith in Jesus. Now, because of this gracious giving of righteousness, there is no distinction between people. We are all the same in our sinfulness and do not match up to the glory of God. But despite our shortcomings, we are made right with God through His sacrifice of atonement (_HILASTĒRION_).

The meaning in these verses is two-fold.

1. Jesus is described in verses 21-24 as the sacrifice given to pay for our sins, and

2. Jesus is described in verse 25 as the actual throne of mercy (the Mercy Seat) where God's approval is given through His blood.

The second meaning can be seen in Romans 3:25a GWT.

> *"God showed that Christ is the throne of mercy where God's approval is given through faith in Christ's blood."*

HILASTĒRION is a word that implies dual meaning. It acknowledges the physical Mercy Seat of the Old Testament tabernacle and refers to the atoning sacrifice upon it. Christ became the Mercy Seat and gained God's approval for us who have faith in His blood. Through this, God proves Himself just for granting grace to the sins of the past, and proves Himself as the ongoing justifier for those who believe in Him.

Remember all of what was done by the tabernacle high priest for atonement within the Most Holy Place was done so the Israelites could be in the presence of the Most High God. Consider, Jesus became the blood of sacrifice and the cover of mercy upon which this sacrificial blood was sprinkled. In every aspect, He became the atonement. Not only that, but He also became the scapegoat who carried their sin to a far away, remote place. Jesus fulfilled, and continues to fulfill, every aspect of what was required to allow God's people to approach Him.

Thank You, Jesus!

Jesus clarified this by His words recorded in Matthew 5:17. Write out this verse below.

_____

_____

Read Hebrews 10:4-10 NIV and fill in the blanks below.

"It is _____ **for the blood of bulls and goats to take away sins." (vs 4)**

Christ said, "Sacrifice and offering you did _____ **desire, but a** _____ **You prepared for me." (vs 5) "...I have come to do** _____ **will, my God." (vs 7)**

"By that will, we have been made _____ **through the** _____ **of the** _____ **of Jesus Christ once for all." (vs 10)**

We have read it before, but take another look at Ephesians 2:13.

What was the condition allowing those who were far away from God to be brought near?

_____

Imagine what it would be like to need to atone for your wrong doings. Imagine going through an elaborate process of paying for your sins, only to be riddled with guilt again the following year if the ritual is not repeated. Imagine never being washed clean for good.

Oh, these thoughts sicken me. Sometimes it is only because I know that my sins are forever removed that I can face my day. The weight of their imagined return is unbearable. Oh, how I love Jesus—the Mercy Seat—who by His mercy, fulfilled every necessary work to allow me to approach the Lord.

Read Hebrews 4:16 and Ephesians 3:12.

How can we, who are aware of our smallness in comparison to this great Savior, approach God's throne?

_____

_____

Our great Savior deserves of our highest reverence. His mercy makes His throne approachable, and thus makes intimacy with Him possible. He allows us to approach Him with confidence. This is not confidence in ourselves or in our righteousness. It is confidence in Him and the revelation of His character of mercy, grace, and unity. This character is so significant it permeates the design of His throne in Heaven, on earth, and in Jesus Himself.

Based on what you've learned today, approach God with boldness. Pour out your reflections in intimate conversation with Him.

_____

_____

_____

_____

_____

_____

_____

_____

The Sacrifice of Atonement - Part 2

- •● ● ●●• -

Key Verse

Romans 3:25a NIV: *"God presented Christ as a sacrifice of atonement, through the shedding of his blood—to be received by faith."*

Yesterday, we finished our lesson by reflecting on the confidence we can have to approach God. I hope you are enjoying new freedom in your faith. Today, I am eager to continue, so let's jump right back into the richness of God's great display of His mercy through Jesus Christ.

Consider the weight of Jesus' commitment to bring to completion His sacrifice of atonement.

Read Luke 22:41-44.

How did Jesus feel about what He was about to do?

_____

Fast forward to the time when Jesus was brought before the elders, chief priests, and the teachers of the law.

Read Luke 22:66-70.

Where did Jesus say that He would be seated from now on?

_____

What truth did Jesus communicate about Himself?

_____

Read John 19:11. In this verse, Jesus reiterates His commitment to the will of His Father in heaven. What was the only power Pilate (and others) had over Jesus?

_____

Read John 19:19-22. What was the debate between Pilate and the chief priests who had spoken with Jesus in Luke 22?

_____

Read John 19:1-3. Name three things done to mock the Kingship of Jesus.

1. _____

2. _____

3. _____

In all the stories of Jesus on earth, there was only once Jesus was crowned, dressed like royalty, and called King—and that was done in absolute mockery. This mocking continued as Jesus hung on the cross.

Read Luke 23:36-37. How did the soldiers suggest Jesus ought to prove His Kingship?

_____

Read Luke 23:34. In contrast to all this mocking, how did Jesus display His mercy?

_____

As Jesus hung high above the onlookers on their throne of mockery, His character was not changed. He offered Himself as a sacrifice for the sins of the people. Jesus lived out His true throne of mercy while hoisted up on their throne of mockery.

If you share my desire to do so, stop here to thank Jesus for what He endured.

_____

_____

_____

_____

Read Matthew 27:45-54 NIV and fill in the blanks below.

Darkness spread over all the land for _____ hours while Jesus hung on the cross. (vs 45)

At about 3 pm Jesus cried out, "My God, my God, why have You _____ me?" (vs 46) "Jesus then _____ _____ His Spirit." (vs 50)

At the moment that Jesus gave up His Spirit something significant happened. "The curtain of the _____ was _____ in two from top to bottom." (vs 51)

The centurion and those guarding Jesus were terrified and concluded that Jesus was the _____ of _____ . (vs 54)

In our previous exploration of the Mercy Seat, we examined the mobile tabernacle the Israelites utilized in the desert. Many years after the Israelites were near Mount Sinai, they were led by David's son, Solomon, to build a structure in Jerusalem which was patterned after the tabernacle, known as the temple.

Within the temple, the Most Holy Place was exactly like the tabernacle. It contained the Ark of the Covenant covered by the Mercy Seat, above which sat the presence of the Lord. In both the tabernacle and the temple, the Most Holy Place was separated from the rest of the structure by a veil or curtain (Exodus 26:33-34).

Remember from yesterday's study, only the high priest could pass this veil to enter the Most Holy Place once a year, and after taking great precautions. The consequence of going beyond the veil was immediate death, as was experienced by Aaron's sons.

Matthew 27:51 tells us that the exact moment Jesus breathed His last breath—the moment His shedding of blood was complete—the veil which separated God's people from His presence was torn in two. The barrier created by our sin, the one no amount of imperfect sacrifice could tear down, was completely destroyed!

Read Hebrews 10:19-23.

According to verse 19, what may we have as we approach God?

_____

Why?

_____

_____

According to verse 22, what should be our response?

_____

_____

What can we hold onto because of Christ's faithfulness? (vs 23)

_____

What does this mean to you? How does this truth impact your intimacy with God?

_____

_____

Following Jesus' death on the cross, He, like the scapegoat, carried the sins of the people to a remote place. Having washed us of our guilt through His perfect blood sacrifice, He opened the veil that had kept His people from approaching the Father with confidence. Jesus' task was to carry out the will of His Father. That will was to reconcile mankind to Himself. With this purpose fulfilled, listen to what followed for Jesus.

Read the following verses.

> **Hebrews 1:3**   **Hebrews 10:12**   **Hebrews 12:2b**

What happened to Jesus when He completed the Father's will on Earth?

_____

As we studied in John 19:11, Jesus stated the only power humans had over Him was given to them by the Father so His will for reconciliation would be accomplished.

What do the following verses tell us about the power of Jesus after God's plan was complete?

Hebrews 10:13-14

_____

Psalm 110:1

_____

1 Corinthians 15:25-28

_____

_____

We learned in our study of intimacy that Jesus gave up everything He was entitled to, in order to take on the humility of man.

Read Philippians 2:9-11 NIV. What is God's reaction to Jesus' humility?

God _____ Him to the highest place (vs 9), and gave Him the name that

is _____ every name (vs 9), that at the name of _____ (vs 10)

every knee should _____ (vs 10), and every tongue _____ that

Jesus Christ is _____ (vs 11), to the _____ of God the Father.

Jesus submitted to the will He and His Father had purposed before He came to earth in human form. He was humbled in every way, gave up His human life, and ripped open a perfect pathway for us to approach God with confidence. Then, He was raised up to heaven where He sits enthroned at the right hand of God, with all authority, as His enemies are made a footstool beneath His feet, and every living being will acknowledge Him for who He is.

Don't you just want to fist pump a little right here! Jesus finally gets what He deserves! After all the mocking, all the pain, all the humility, all the meekness He endured on my behalf, on your behalf, Jesus is exalted and no one will miss it! There is not a single mocker, not a single fake crown, no false robe, no jeering taunts of "Save yourself," or "You're the king of the Jews."

Oh Father, I thank You for exalting Jesus! He deserves it. Thank You for rescuing us and making a way for us to approach You with confidence. Thank You the story doesn't end there. Thank You that, although He endured pain, mocking, Your wrath upon sin, and the burden of being a scapegoat, He is not exiled forever. Thank You for being just. Thank You for being faithful. Thank You no enemy of Yours can reign over Your beloved Son. I join with the chorus of tongues acknowledging Jesus Christ as our Lord and Lord of all!

Pray your thoughts and feelings to God about these truths.

_____

_____

_____

_____

_____

Imagine again the throne of God Ezekiel saw in heaven. Picture all its splendor. Picture the vast vault sparkling like crystal, the throne representing royalty, honor, wisdom and trust, the fiery figure of a man sitting above it, and the rainbow of mercy surrounding it. Soak in the awe and reverence that flows from this glimpse of our majestic and powerful God.

Now picture Jesus seated at God's right hand, with all authority, and with every enemy locked beneath His feet. Upon His seat in heaven there is no mockery. Every knee is bowed, every tongue confesses, He is the Lord.

Write out Revelation 3:21.

_____

_____

_____

Allow the truth of your position as a believer to enter this picture. You are forgiven. You are healed. As a believer, you are on Jesus' right, positioned to take your inheritance. Because of the power that raised Him from the dead, you are victorious, an overcomer, and just as Jesus was raised up, you also are granted a seat on Jesus' throne. Can you imagine a more overwhelming scene of reverence and intimacy?

What does this mean to you?

_____

_____

_____

Talk to God about the devotion you feel toward Him, as a result of His actions.

_____

_____

_____

_____

_____

_____

Dive Deeper 5

- ·•●•·-

Give Me Wisdom, O God

Write out James 1:5.

_____

_____

_____

_____

_____

_____

Pray for Readiness to Learn from God

┌─ *Example* ─────────────────────────────┐

Lord, Your word says I can ask You for wisdom, so here I am asking. Thank You for being generous without finding fault in my limited abilities to understand all You possess. Please teach me. I want Your wisdom as I study Your Word. Thank You for Your Holy Spirit who resides inside me.

└───┘

You can pray along with this sample prayer or write one below to better communicate your thoughts and feelings.

_____

_____

_____

_____

_____

_____

Listen and Confess

Be patient. Sit and wait before God. Listen to what rattles around in your mind and in your heart. Do you sense any conviction of sin, awareness of distraction, or impeding negativity? If so, confess these to God.

_____

_____

Review

With hindrances laid aside, ask God to lead you as you review the material from this week. Please do not skip this part, thinking you've already done the work. Learning to learn from God, to be open to His personal instruction, and to seek His voice are rich and deep blessings. I pray you will not settle for your experience of God to remain indirect, learning only through others. God will mentor you—what a thrill!

Write out the key scripture verse for each lesson this week. Then, highlight the main point you learned day by day. Make your reflections personal.

Day 1 & 2: The Mercy Seat

Exodus 25:22

_____

_____

_____

Your Main Learning Point: Day 1

_____

_____

Your Main Learning Point: Day 2

_____

_____

_____

Day 3 & 4: Sacrifice of Atonement

Romans 3:25a

_____

_____

_____

Your Main Learning Point: Day 3

_____

_____

_____

Your Main Learning Point: Day 4

_____

_____

_____

Study Skills

Comparing Bible Translations

In Bible translation, biblical scholars study the original Hebrew (Old Testament) and Greek (New Testament) scriptures and set out to convey the intended message to English readers.

Some Bible translations examine each word one at a time, while others tackle phrases. Word-for-word translations offer accuracy and precision with individual words, whereas phrase-by-phrase translations give insight into cultural nuances and figures of speech that would be lost in the translation of each word without the surrounding words.

The key verses studied this week can be examined in word-for-word versions or phrase-by-phrase. To read different translations can add depth of understanding to any given text because they expand the reader's comprehension of the full connotation.

Let's check this out together on the internet. If you do not have internet access, Christian book stores have multiple Bible translations on their shelves.

Go to www.biblegateway.com.

In the search bar at the top of the page, type in Exodus 25:22 and use the drop-down bar to the right to select the NIV translation. Press the search icon. The verse will appear below the search bar.

When the verse is visible, look for the page-related icons on the right-hand side of the page. There is a blue rectangle that says, "Related Resources" and directly below it there are icons that (when the mouse hovers over them) say, "Share" "Print" "Page Options" "Add Parallel" and "Listen". Click the "Add Parallel" icon. Another version of the same verse will appear in a column beside the original one. Press the "Add Parallel" icon 3 times so that 4 different versions of this verse show in columns across your screen.

You can explore as many different versions as you'd like by clicking on the version and making a new selection from the drop-down menu.

The Bible version I study most often is the NASB, but I have spent seasons enjoying the NIV, NLT, MSG, AMP, and EXB (to name a few). Each version offers something different. The NASB is a word-for-word translation that uses older English, but it's not as difficult to understand as the KJV. The NIV is a well-known word-for-word translation. The NLT and MSG are phrase-by-phrase translations that assist my understanding. The AMP and EXB are word-for-word translations that list synonyms for some words to convey a deeper ambiance. I hope you have fun exploring the great options available.

> The Bible can be explored using a word-for-word or phrase-by-phrase translation. Either way, while you read, seek to understand truth, not discover a loophole.

When utilizing various versions, please also use discernment. Talk with God about what you are reading. Ask His Holy Spirit to aid you in your perception of truth. If you come across a version that seems to communicate a different message than the rest, be cautious. Check it out further. Seek the counsel of someone you trust for their knowledge of the word. Check your motivation. If four versions say, "Honor your mother and father," and you persist in your search of other translations because you aspire to lash out at your mom, there is a problem. When you explore, seek to understand truth, not discover a loophole.

Ok, let's get on with it.

Exodus 25:22

With four versions of Exodus 25:22 on your screen, consider the differences. Record the version examined and the disparity you notice.

Bible Version	**Differences**
_____	_____
_____	_____
_____	_____
_____	_____

What insights do you gain from reading this verse in other translations?

_____

_____

If anything confuses or concerns you about the wording in one of the versions, record it below.

_____

_____

_____

Express your thoughts and feelings about this process to God.

_____

_____

_____

_____

_____

_____

Romans 3:25

Now repeat these steps with the second verse from this week.

With four versions of Romans 3:25 on your screen, consider the differences. Record the version examined and the disparity you notice.

Bible Version	Differences
_____	_____
_____	_____
_____	_____
_____	_____

What insights do you gain from reading this verse in other translations?

_____

_____

If anything confuses or concerns you about the wording in one of the versions, record it below.

_____

_____

Express your thoughts and feelings about this process to God.

_____

_____

_____

_____

_____

_____

> *Thanks Lord for teaching us through Your Spirit and Word. You are gracious and kind to us. You bless us with Your presence and Your guidance. Help us to use the tools available to run toward You, not hide from You. We want You, Lord. Give each of us a hunger to depend on Your greatness, to submit to Your ways, and worship You fully. Please grant us a great thirst to seek You, to know You, and to love You. You are worth every moment, Lord!*

Week 6

Step into Abundant Life

Lesson 6

Filled

· · ● ● ● ● · ·

Head on over to www.lisadevries.ca/bigfreshfaith/
→ **Watch the Video Lessons** → **Watch Lesson 6 and follow along below.**

●·· In each era of God's interaction with man, He is _____ as King

and _____ with His people.

●·· God _____ man was cause for great hoopla.

A Great Hoopla

●·· Each instance when the _____ of God was made known, His presence

intimately _____ the place, and they experienced the impetus to move intimately

_____ _____ with God.

God's Current Dwelling Place

●·· On the day of your salvation, the _____ of the Lord burst forth and _____

you just as He did the tabernacle and temple, and in the sky when Jesus came.

●·· You and I, who live by faith in Christ, have God _____ in us, just as He dwelt in these

places we've studied this week.

Ephesians 1:13-14 NLT:

*"When you believed in Christ, He identified you as His own by giving you the _____ ,
whom He promised long ago. The Spirit is God's guarantee that He will give us the inheritance
He promised and that He has purchased us to be His own people. He did this so we would praise
and glorify Him."*

●·· Because of the indwelling of the Holy Spirit, we are the beneficiaries of the closest,

most _____ dwelling place of God throughout the history of man.

Suggestions for Prayer

· Talk to God about what stirs in you from this lesson.

· Ask God something as if He were standing right beside you. Be watchful and attentive for His response
as you go about your week.

· Praise God for His willingness to make you His dwelling place.

Created

┌─── **Key Verse** ──────────────────────────────┐

Psalm 139:16 NIV: "Your eyes saw my unformed body; all the days ordained
for me were written in your book before one of them came to be."

└── ·•●•· ┘

Bonded through mischief and fun, my brother and I grew up as thick as thieves. Our days were full of adventure and banter. Being a year older, he made me feel like the most important kid in the world. He chose me first in school yard picks and threw his weight around if any boy disagreed. He laughed at my jokes, affirmed my ideas, and refused to raise the bar of excellence until I succeeded. I couldn't dream of a better brother.

Sadly, as adults, we live on opposite sides of the continent, so we see each other less than we'd like. I anticipate those visits with enthusiasm, knowing we will pick up right where we left off. I giggle to myself often when we are together because my brother and I share some family traits unique to the two of us. At the top of the list, we are somewhat disorganized, always running a little late, and never without a lofty idea. When I see these personality quirks in my brother I feel understood—like I belong somewhere. It's a great feeling, even though these traits are kind of stressful, and on many occasions, a headache for the people around us.

The last time I was with him I wondered where these traits come from. My mom and my sister are the opposite—organized, punctual and steady-minded. The question, as I shake my head and laugh, is why are we such *wing-nuts*?

My dad died when I was five years old. My brother was only six. Neither of us remember a lot about his personality, so I wonder if we are like him. I have a vague memory of him hustling me off to kindergarten in a flap because we were late. I like it a lot. I've been told he was always moving from one big idea to the next. Hearing that is music to my ears. Both my dad's parents have long passed away, but I wish I could ask them all kinds of questions so I could know if there are more ways my brother and I are like him.

This searching, this desire to know the one whose image I may bear, hasn't subsided in the decades since he died. I don't know why it is like this. I just know the desire to know my gene pool is strong. In the past, I worked with kids who were in foster care and adoptive homes, and I heard so many of them express this too. I've concluded curiosity about who we come from is natural and persistent.

Of late, I've been asking myself this question: "Am I as curious about how my appearance, my personality, and my behaviors resemble those of my Father in heaven, as I am about my resemblance to my dad?"

Are you as curious about your resemblance to your Heavenly Father as you are about your resemblance to your parents or your children?

Made in Their Likeness

When it comes to family traits, our heavenly Father and His beloved Son take the cake.

Read Hebrews 1:1-3 and answer the following questions.

Who is the radiance of God's glory? (vs 3)

_____

How does He resemble the Father? (vs 3)

_____

Read Colossians 1:15.

The Son is the _____ of the invisible God, the firstborn over all creation.

Jesus displayed the radiance of His Father's glory. He is the exact replica of His Father's being, and is the image-bearer of the God whom we cannot see. The passing on of DNA is perfect.

Read John 14:6-11. Check all the things Jesus said about His resemblance to the Father.

_____ **If you know me, you will know my Father as well.**

_____ **My body looks just like my Father's**

_____ **Anyone who has seen me has seen the Father.**

_____ **I am in the Father, and the Father is in me.**

_____ **I have the same color eyes as my Father.**

_____ **I do not speak with my authority, rather it is the Father living in me, who is doing His work.**

Jesus' disciples wanted to know the Father. Jesus explained that knowing Him meant knowing the Father. The resemblance is so exact that when the disciples saw and heard Jesus, they were getting to know the Father. The reason given for this perfect likeness was that the Father, in all His power, was residing in Jesus and vice versa.

When Jesus was sent to earth, He came to reflect and reveal His Father. He came to make the invisible, visible.

Created Design

Listen to what we're told in the first half of Genesis 1:26 NIV.

"Then God said, 'Let us make mankind in our _____ , in our _____ ..."

Likeness: TSELEM (H6754)

The word translated as, likeness, in Genesis 1:26 means to bear the image of, to be alike, to be a representative figure, or a model of another.

Our God—Father, Son, and Holy Spirit—invented and crafted mankind in Their image and likeness. Just as They planned for Jesus to be a representation of God to mankind, They planned for humans to be representative figures for the unseen image of God. Wow, right?

Now go with me for a minute here. I want you to call to mind an elaborate filing system. It could be a big Craftsman workbench with a thousand tiny, pull-out drawers, or maybe a craft cupboard that organizes all your specific supplies into separate compartments. Get a visual, in your mind's eye, of something like that.

Picture each of those drawers or storage compartments with a label. The label is marked with a trait that belongs to God. It could be mercy, love, wisdom, or faithfulness. It could be marked with any quality true to the Lord's character.

Brainstorm some qualities God possesses. List them below.

_____   _____   _____

_____   _____   _____

_____   _____   _____

_____   _____   _____

Ok, your list won't be exhaustive, but hopefully you've got some ideas written down.

Now, imagine the day of your creation. God ponders over how He will craft you. He is about to make decisions about your personality, your demeanor, your voice, your gait, your mind. He will design you from head to toe, inside and out.

Imagine as God sets out to form you, He looks at all those tiny drawers of His own traits, and begins to choose which of them He will plant inside you. If we could have listed every trait of God, those drawers would be His entire repertoire of options. There is nothing God chooses to be part of your created identity that does not come from His identity.

Reflect on this. You are created in the image of the Lord. There was nothing chosen for you that was inferior, broken or embarrassing. The only qualities and features chosen to make you had to come from His image, otherwise He could not say you are His likeness. To have other options would make you unlike Him, which is not scripturally accurate.

You were made to resemble God. How does this truth impact you?

_____

_____

_____

Read Psalm 139:13-16.

What indicates the Lord was intimately involved in how you were made?

_____

_____

_____

God fashioned Jesus as an exact imprint of His nature so we could see the invisible God. He also, at creation, fashioned you and I to be like Him. He took the traits and qualities present in Himself and formed them into people—you and I, and everyone we know.

Given Life

Read Genesis 2:7 to hear what happened next. Circle the correct answer below.

God formed man and then:
a. **had a party**
b. **had a rest**
c. **breathed a sigh of relief**
d. **breathed life into him**

Isaiah 42:5 describes God as One who gives breath and life to those who walk on the earth. God formed man in His image, then gave life to him. He did this to humanity in general, but also to you and I, specifically. This is good news to us, but it is also intended to be good news for God.

For God's Glory

We read Colossians 1:15 earlier in our lesson. Now jump to Colossians 1:17 NIV.

"[Jesus] is _____ all things, and in Him all things _____

_____ ."

Read John 1:1-3 NIV.

This passage references Jesus as the Word. It credits Him with making all things.

Verse 3 states, "Through Him _____ things were made, and that without

Him, _____ has been made."

Read Isaiah 43:7. What reason is given for creating us?

_____

God created us for His glory. Jesus was the perfect model of God. Just as He was patterned after God, He was active in creation to pattern us after God. God did this to reveal His invisible nature to the whole world.

Romans 11:36 tells us, "From Him and through Him and to Him are all things." For this reason, we attribute glory, praise, and honor to the Lord forever.

What is the reason given, in Revelation 4:11, for God to receive glory, honor, and power?

_____

You and I, and Jesus, were given human form so God would be glorified. God put His unseen beauty in skin, and chose to give us life, so we would see Him, know Him and glorify Him.

How does God's design of you, His image in you, and His desire to receive glory through you, impact you today?

_____
_____
_____
_____
_____

If there are parts of your created design you dislike or have trouble accepting, please spend time talking with God about them.

_____
_____
_____
_____
_____
_____

If it is congruent for you, confess your rejection of God's trait selection for you.

_____
_____
_____
_____

Ask God to help you take to heart the truths revealed about your design. Ask Him to make you curious about how you were made to resemble Him. Ask Him to stir in you the natural and persistent desire to know how you are like your Father.

_____

_____

_____

_____

_____

How could understanding God's intention and design help you dive into abundant life?

_____

_____

_____

_____

How can you steward God's creation of you? Ask God to show you a way you can put your faith in Him into action. Wait, listen and watch for Him to respond throughout the week.

_____

_____

_____

_____

_____

_____

_____

Day 2

Purposed

—··•●•··—

— Key Verse —

Ephesians 2:10 ESV: *"For we are his workmanship, created in Christ Jesus for good works, which God prepared beforehand, that we should walk in them."*

I'm happy to be back to study together again today.

Lord, I pray we will be led and taught by You. I pray Your sovereignty over every letter written here, and every prompt that occurs in the hearts and minds of those who read it. Please carry out Your will, Your way, for Your purpose among us.

Creation was our topic yesterday. I hope you have reflected on your likeness to your Father and delighted in His intention to imprint His qualities in you. There is purpose in God's decision to make us in His image. He displays His invisible qualities through us, so He may be glorified. Today, we will examine His purposes for us. Not only His purpose in creation, but His purpose in every moment of our lives. I hope you sense the beauty of your identity and anticipate learning more about your purpose.

God's Plan

I can think of many followers of Christ who are convinced they are called to do a specific job for the kingdom of God. I thank God for the clarity they have and for their faithfulness to live it out. What a wonderful gift given to each of them. However, not everybody feels this way.

From the perspective of "right answers," many Christians say, "Amen" to the notion that God has a plan for their lives, but in all candor, these same believers may struggle to see how their lives fit in God's great plans for the world.

The following testimony was written by my son at a time when he grappled with this question. He said I could share it with you.

"I am 12 years old. I was raised in a Christian home, and learned about God through my whole life. When I was younger, I loved reading the Bible and singing songs about God. God seemed to be the answer to all my questions.

But lately, I have lots of questions. I go to church, but my mind wanders. I feel bored. I like hanging out and playing games with my friends at youth, but I don't really know how it relates to God. I'm supposed to read my Bible, but the novels I get from the library are way more interesting.

I'm not sure what this means about me. Maybe I never really knew God. I accepted Jesus when I was so young, maybe it wasn't real. When I read the Bible, I don't know what to do. I go to school, play sports, hang out with my friends, but does it matter to God?

Someone told me I'm supposed to live like Christ. Then, if I do, maybe someone'll ask why I am different. Then I can tell them about Jesus. Problem though…no one asks me that. In my whole life, I've never told anyone about Jesus. It's weird.

I pray for my food, my safety, and the kids we sponsor. I pray for my coach who doesn't know Jesus, and ask God to forgive me when I get in trouble. But I don't even know if God hears me. I can't tell.

I thought being a Christian would be different, but I don't see any difference between me and everybody else."

I have heard this familiar cry from so many hearts. It begs to know we matter in the kingdom of God. I hear the question in the voice of youth, but I also hear it out of the mouths of 30, 50, 70-year-old believers who have spent their lives going to church, praying, reading their Bible, and giving to those in need.

Purposed for Good Works

Let's start with our key verse for today. Please read it and circle the best answer below.

We are God's:	a. hope	b. joy	c. stressors	d. workmanship
We were created in:	a. Christ	b. hope	c. joy	d. stress
We were created for:	a. good times	b. good works	c. good pleasure	

Fill in the blanks from the last portion of the key verse.

- …which God _____ beforehand

- …that we should _____ in them.

I get so excited about the truths in God's word! I hope you are right there with me.

In yesterday's homework, we learned we were created by God, in Christ, and with intention. Here we are called His workmanship. I think of a carpenter friend of mine who takes incredible care with his work. It is his craft. It matters to him how his work turns out. He will refine until he is pleased. Same it is with our God and His craftsmanship. He didn't slop us together. We are intricate.

Listen for purpose. We were created for good works prepared before our lives began. Way back, when God was considering our creation, He was not haphazard. He had full knowledge of every good work He would ask us to participate in. At the time you were being created, God not only chose your characteristics out of qualities He possesses, He chose your characteristics based on what He would ask you to do.

You see, there is no chance of surprising God. He knows all things, through all time. You were not made in ignorance of what you would face in your life. You were made as a reflection of the invisible God, who had every moment of your future played out in His mind at the specific moment He was forming you out of a pile of dust. Isn't that wild?

God, with all His foreknowledge, had a purpose in mind for the package He put together in you. He knew what lay ahead. He knew what you would need to live through it. He knew what you would need not only to survive, but to carry out the plans He had already prepared for you. God did not miss anything, which confirms you and I are not flawed in design or purpose. Let that sink in for a moment.

> God not only chose your characteristics out of qualities He possesses, He also chose them based on what He would ask you to do. Does this impact your confidence in serving God?

How would your life change if you believed there was no mistake in how you were put together?

_____

_____

_____

How would your life change if you believed you were put together to carry out the purposes God planned out in advance for you?

_____

_____

_____

Participation

The last part of the key verse says all the creation and planning hoopla has been put into motion so we will participate in it. The EXB version of the Bible, words the purpose in this last section of Ephesians 2:10 as "for us to live our lives doing." Therefore, God created us and planned actions for us to do so we can live our lives doing them.

God never intended for us to be created and then feel all alone to figure out what we ought to do with our existence. Creation and purpose go hand in hand.

What do the following verses teach about God's plans and purposes?

Proverbs 16:4 _____

Jeremiah 29:11 _____

Romans 8:28 _____

You and I are not the exceptions to these verses. God has plans for us. He has intentions for every creation, including those who oppose Him. In all cases, God works out the purposes He set out before the world was formed. Confidence in this truth can bring meaning to our days. It can bring hope and newness to faith.

How do the following verses foster confidence in the Lord's plans?

Psalm 138:8

_____

_____

Isaiah 55:11

_____

_____

Isaiah 46:10-11

_____

_____

Job 42:2

_____

_____

The Lord will fulfill. The Lord will accomplish. He will do it. No plan of His can be thwarted!

Discuss with God your confidence, or lack thereof, in Him to come through in the plans He laid out for you.

_____

_____

_____

_____

_____

_____

These truths challenge. Sometimes it seems the fall of man interfered with God's plans. When we, or someone we love, encounters life-limiting sickness, or death, or devastating hurt, or the wickedness of sin, God's sovereignty can sting. It causes us to wrestle with why, if God is in control, such things ever happen.

There are many moments in my life where God's plans seemed to be thwarted. I have had seasons of great anger toward God over His apparent lack of action. My inability to see Him fulfilling, accomplishing, and doing, when I know He has the power to, has at times, felt like daggers sent straight to my heart. Times like these have tried my faith with intensity.

Have you ever struggled to accept God's sovereignty in the midst of what was happening in your life? If so, reflect on what that time was like for you.

_____

_____

_____

_____

Read Philippians 2:12-13 NIV.

Verse 12 tells us to _____ _____ our salvation with fear and trembling.

This instruction to work out our salvation means to tend to it, to be active in pursuit of spiritual maturity. As we've learned throughout this study, this pursuit of spiritual maturity is synonymous with the purification of our faith. It is through faith in Christ, we are saved. And living by faith requires some working out or wrestling from time to time because it is hard.

It is hard when God's ways don't make sense to us. It is hard when we don't like what He allows. It is hard when the brokenness in this world presses against us. We are not told to pretend it's all okay, and to pray with good manners to God. We are instructed to get in there and work it out with intimate authenticity while revering God with fear and trembling.

Faith is worth it. There is no way to thrive in the purposes God has for us if our faith can't handle the muddled perspective of our humanness. Faith is knowing something with such confidence it impacts what we think, feel, and do. When we do not know truth, when we struggle to believe truth, or when we flat out disagree with truth, our faith will falter. So, when we get stuck with the difficulty of submitting to God's ways, we must persevere to work it out through faith. Ignoring our questions or pretending they don't exist does not allow us to move forward with a big, fresh faith.

Now focus on verse 13 NIV to fill in the blanks.

"For it is God who works in you to _____ and to _____ in order to fulfill his good purpose."

God created you to reflect Him, and He has plans for you. He promises to come alongside you and work in you so you fulfill His good purpose. Incredible, right? The Lord will accomplish, He will not be thwarted, and He orchestrates all things so the hearts, minds and actions of faithful believers move in sync with Him.

Through prayer to God, work out your thoughts and feelings about His purposes for you.

_____

_____

_____

_____

_____

_____

_____

If you, like my son, have struggled with faith because your purpose seems undetectable, be honest with God about how you feel. Ask Him to show you how your creation matches with what He wants you to do. If you struggle to understand this, start by telling Him that.

_____

_____

_____

_____

_____

_____

_____

It is a challenge to let these truths sink in to the depth that enables us to live the abundant life the Lord has for us. How will these truths impact your living?

_____

_____

_____

_____

_____

_____

_____

Equipped

- ·•● ●·· -

2 Thessalonians 1:11 MSG: "...We...pray that our God will make you fit for what
he's called you to be, pray that he'll fill your good ideas and acts of faith with his own energy
so that it all amounts to something."

- ·•● ●·· -

So far this week, we have studied the beautiful cohesion between God's creation of us and His purpose for us. I hope you have been encouraged by God's intentionality, and I hope you work out the questions that arise as you navigate this material.

Today's lesson is one of my favorites. We are going to study how we are enabled to walk in step with the purposes God has for us. Let's check this out.

We are equipped to engage with the Lord's plans in three ways.
1. We are given authority
2. The Holy Spirit empowers us
3. Jesus intercedes for us

We are Given Authority

When Jesus was on earth, He taught about the authority of God.

Read John 14:10. On whose authority did Jesus speak?

_____

Read Matthew 28:18 NIV and fill in the blank below.

- **"Then Jesus came to them and said, 'All _____ in heaven and on earth has been given to Me.'"**

Read Luke 4:32. Why were people impressed with Jesus?

_____

Jesus spoke with the authority of God and people took notice. His was not a limited authority, but the full authority of the God of the universe.

In Luke 10, Jesus sent out 72 of His followers to do the work of the Lord. He told them to speak of the kingdom of God and to heal the sick. The 72 went out and did as He instructed. When they returned, they were full of joy.

Read Luke 10:17-19.

Why were the 72 full of joy?
    a. People had given them gifts
    b. They had fun
    c. Demons submitted to them in Jesus' name
    d. They were well fed

Why did demons submit to them in Jesus' name? (vs 19)

_____

Jesus was equipped with the authority of His Father, and when His followers participated in His purposes, He gave them the same authority. The great and wonderful God who is enthroned in heaven has entrusted those who follow His Son with His authority! That means you and I, if we are followers of Jesus, have been given His authority too.

Who are we, Lord, that You would do such a thing?

The Holy Spirit Empowers Us

When Jesus told His disciples He would return to His Father in heaven, the disciples were upset. Jesus tried to explain the benefits, but they were filled with grief.

Read John 16:7.

What was the good thing that would happen for the disciples if Jesus went away?

_____

Review John 14:26 and Acts 1:8, and circle the right answer below.

What good would come from the Holy Spirit being sent?
    a. You will be taught
    b. You will be reminded of Jesus' teachings
    c. You will receive power
    d. You will be Jesus' witnesses
    e. All of the above

Jesus was willing to leave His disciples because there was a better thing coming. He knew when He left, the Holy Spirit would come to each believer to teach them, remind them, empower them, and equip them to be witnesses for the Lord. This exchange—of Jesus in human form for the Holy Spirit—was essential for the good news of salvation to spread throughout the world.

Jesus was limited by His human form. He could not be everywhere in every moment and still be human. The Holy Spirit, on the other hand, does not have this limitation. He can be with every follower in every moment, any place on earth.

Sometimes believers long to have lived in Jesus' time because He was visible, but because He existed in human form, He could never be as close to us as the Holy Spirit is. One human cannot take up residence in another. As we already learned, the Holy Spirit dwells within the believer when Jesus is professed as Lord. This great exchange benefited each of us as individuals and was beneficial for the kingdom of God.

Jesus Intercedes for Us

When Jesus said He was going to return to the Father, He promised He would send the Holy Spirit to His followers. He also made a promise about His ongoing relationship with His disciples.

Read John 14:12-14 NIV and fill in the blanks.

"Very truly I tell you, whoever believes in me will _____ the works I have been doing, and they will do even _____ _____ than these, because _____ am going to the Father. And _____ will do whatever you ask in my _____ , so that the Father may be glorified in the Son. You may ask me for anything in my name, and _____ _____ _____ _____ ."

Jesus promised He would go to the Father, and because of this, His name could be called upon in prayer. In 1 John 2:1, Jesus is described as being with the Father in Heaven, acting as our advocate, counsellor and helper.

Read Hebrews 7:22-25 NIV and fill in the blanks below.

"But because Jesus _____ forever, He has a permanent priesthood. Therefore, He is able to save completely those who come to God through Him, because He always _____ to _____ for them."

Reflecting on these two passages, Jesus did not leave the disciples and let the Holy Spirit take over so He could rest. Jesus went to the Father with purpose. He sent the Spirit to dwell intimately with His followers, and He went to His position, at the right-hand of God, as the permanent Priest in heaven. Jesus died to intercede for us and Jesus lives to intercede for us. He is our advocate before God, both for salvation and in our moments of need. When we pray in Jesus' name, He reiterates our requests to God as though they are His.

What is the significance of Jesus interceding on your behalf when you pray?

_____

_____

_____

_____

Please notice Jesus did not advertise that He would be at our beck and call, like a mindless genie. He gave His disciples—those who committed their lives to His cause—three main assurances.

1. Because they need His authority to carry out His will, they have it.
2. Because they need His power to carry out His will, they have it.
3. And because they need His intercession to carry out His will, they have it forever.

Our Lord has equipped us!

> *Oh Jesus, Your design is perfect. You created us in Your image and for Your glory. You purposed for us to participate in Your plans. You figured out what we would need to join with You, and then fashioned each of us with intention, from the beginning. Then Lord, You knew we couldn't do anything without You, so You died to take away the division of our shortcomings, and shared Your authority and power with us through Your Spirit. As if that isn't more than we could imagine, You sit beside the Father petitioning for us as we encounter our limitations on earth. You are an awesome God. You are deserving of our highest applause. You are beautiful!*

Look back at our key verse for today.

Paul prays for believers in Thessalonica. Imagine his request as it goes up to Jesus in heaven. Then, picture Jesus stamping it with His name, and relaying it to the Father. Jesus listens to Paul's heart and endorses his desire to the Father. It's so cool. Now imagine your last conversation with God. It's incredible to think of Jesus doing the same for us.

"Father, please make _____ **(your name) fit for what You've called her to be.**

Please fill _____ **'s (your name) good ideas and acts of faith with Your own**

energy, God, so that it all amounts to something."

Share your thoughts and feelings with God about how He equips you through Jesus' authority, the Spirit's empowerment, and Jesus' intercession.

_____

_____

_____

_____

_____

_____

_____

_____

Our anticipation for Jesus to come through on His promises is essential to living by faith. If He fails to be who He says He is or do what He says He will do, we are 100% hooped. For me, it's a risk worth taking because the One I am banking on is the King of all Kings.

The question is, do you believe Him? Not just, do you say you believe Him, but do you trust Him? Would you put your life on the line with hope He would come through as Lord? Would you step out to do something that requires His character to be true, or His promises to be kept? Be assured, you will face your worst-case scenario if He fails you.

Write your response to these questions below.

_____

_____

_____

_____

_____

_____

_____

We do not need to run off to closed country riddled with persecution in order to demonstrate faith like this. Sure, some are called to, but I am not talking about some exclusive faith that belongs to missionaries and pastors. I am talking about the private moments in your life and the everyday interactions with family, friends, and strangers.

If I have all the power and authority that raised Jesus from the dead living inside me, and Jesus petitioning for me to walk in the plans He laid out for me, I must live differently as a result. Being equipped by God with His power, authority and intercession, should impact everything I do, everything I say, and everything I think and feel.

I do not intend to point a finger or be a source of condemnation toward any brother or sister of mine. Rather, I hunger for each of you to have the abundant life Jesus promises through faith in Him (John 10:10). To share what God has taught me, I must emphasize that abundant life doesn't come through a mental gesture of faith. Abundant life is the result of faith thriving in the midst of real living. This kind of faith needs reverence for God to get us moving and intimacy with God to sustain us while we go.

> You are equipped by God with His power and authority, and He is interceding for you. You are girded up to succeed in what God calls you to do. With this equipping, are you ready to step out in faith?

Consider these examples.

1. No one is around and you're stressed. Temptation comes to seek escape through overeating, getting a buzz from alcohol, or reading a steamy novel. What you believe in that moment will determine your actions. Complacency might say, "What's the big deal...just a little...who wouldn't," but faith sounds different. Faith says, "I have all the power and authority of Jesus Christ living in me. I want to revere Him with my choices. He is ready to intercede for me because I need His help to resist. I want to be intimate with Him in this." These perspectives would produce different behavior.

2. You just found out your husband looked at pornography again. Despair washes over you. There is a haunting message that declares you are not enough for him. Self-loathing may say, "If you could lose some weight or be more exciting in bed, maybe you'd satisfy him," but faith sounds distinct. Faith claims you were created with intention, purposed for even this moment, and equipped to work this through with the Holy Spirit's assistance in each step.

3. You are trying to determine what direction you should take in your career. It is exciting, yet full of potential insecurities. Worry says, "What if you make the wrong choice? What if you make a mistake? What if this move costs you everything?" In contrast, faith says, "The Lord gives me authority to act in accordance with Him. The Lord gives me power to discern His will. The Lord intercedes on my behalf so I can walk in the plans He laid out for me."

These can sound like pat answers. It's so hard to give a genuine voice to faith when people say these kind of things, yet lived disempowered. I'm not talking about giving the "right answer". I'm talking about knowing it—deep in your soul—such that it changes how you feel, think, and act.

Write an example from your own experience. Try to capture the difference between the messages of doubt, worry, and disempowerment you may be familiar with, and the truths you've been learning.

_____

_____

_____

_____

_____

_____

_____

_____

_____

Do you believe you are equipped with Jesus' authority, the Holy Spirit's power, and Jesus' intercession? Would you put your hopes, your ego, even your life on the line because you trust this truth?

_____

_____

_____

_____

The challenge is to live like these truths are really true. Ask God to show you opportunities to live as though you are equipped by Him.

_____

_____

_____

_____

_____

_____

_____

_____

_____

Victorious

·•◦●◦•·

┌─ *Key Verse* ──

James 1:22 NIV: *"Do not merely listen to the word, and so deceive yourselves. Do what it says."*

─────────────────────────────────·•◦●◦•·─┘

Please take a few minutes to pray before we get started today. Ask God to open your heart to all He has to teach you today.

_____

_____

_____

_____

_____

_____

_____

So far this week, we've focused on the Lord's work in His creation of you, His purposes for you, and His equipping of you. He has gone to great lengths to ensure you are free to live the abundant life He's planned for you.

The Heart of the Challenge

Throughout the homework this week, there has been a sense of challenge with these truths. Each day, I've pushed you to examine how the material will affect your living. There is a place of angst in me as we approach these questions because I don't want to be misunderstood as someone who expects people to get it together. That is the farthest angle from my heart.

I once read the testimony of a woman whom Jesus saved from alcoholism and homelessness. She said something that stuck with me. She said her freedom was linked to her servanthood. She explained that the opportunity to serve with God—to participate with Him in His plans—was critical to her freedom. The reason her words penetrated me, is because she expressed something I had lived, but couldn't put into words.

I have been in extensive bondage. I have loved God and been racked and beaten by the enemy at the same time. I have been desperate for God while rejecting His help. I have been so abused by the rebelliousness of my own flesh I lost hope toward free life. I am a sinner saved only by the deep, wonderful, life-giving grace of my Savior.

I was pursued by my God, loved when I had nothing to offer Him in return and restored to a life and inheritance I will never deserve. Every day, I am amazed at the great chasm between what I ought to have and what I actually have. It fills my heart with overflowing gratitude because there is nothing I did to earn any of it. Quite the opposite, what I earned, I never received.

Just as this saved woman expressed, if I could not express my thankfulness to the Lord in action, my faith would falter. My freedom would die. My vitality would shrivel up. You see, I need to move with the Lord. I cannot make it on my own. I need to see Him in action. I can't cope with complacency or going through the motions of faith, because I don't see evidence of Him there. Theologically, I know He is everywhere, but the revelation of Him to me is rich when I engage in the things He has instructed me to do.

> Do you find yourself hungry to see God in action? Does His movement in and around you act as a lifeline for your faith?

In no way did servanthood save me or bring me victory. I was sinning, not serving, when God intervened. Since being given victory in Christ, however, servanthood is crucial for me to continue in it. Please understand this point. Servanthood is doing what Jesus is doing, moving where the Spirit tells us to move. The reason participating in God's work is so critical is because it provides an up-close view of God in action. My faith needs to see that so I don't crumble under the intimidation of life!

I know myself enough to admit I need a frequent, fresh supply of proof God is living and active. If I want to see this proof, I must step out in faith! You see, when I'm in the business of doing what Jesus loves, I see vibrant evidence of Him and my faith grows. This, in turn, gives me courage and strength to trust Him. Then confidence in Him allows me to live victoriously moment to moment.

I want others to know there is freedom in faith. I want to shout from the mountain tops that when you seek Jesus, He will be found by you. He will be found in salvation, but He will also be found in a million moments of every day. He is busy at work and He welcomes us to join in with Him. He has purposed us to do just that.

I am convinced faith, the real and active kind, needs to be in motion to stay fresh. Every time we step out in faith, we have the opportunity to be aware of our nearness to God in action. If we are expecting Him to be who He says He is and do what He says He'll do, we need to see Him come through on a regular basis. The only way that is going to happen is if we follow Him out to where we experience our need for Him.

Have you ever had an experience where you knew your servanthood was a front row seat to see God at work? If so, how did servanthood build your faith?

_____

_____

_____

_____

_____

Faith Without Works is Dead

Read James 2:14-26. Write out verse 17 below.

Remember these verses from our first lesson together? Faith forging ahead is not the same as fraudulent faith.

Faith without action is like playing the drums on an air guitar, or like a paper tiger trying to take down an elephant. Faith without action is like swimming in oxygen without the two molecules of hydrogen. If you are confused, don't worry, it's the point. These concepts don't make any sense. They aren't real. The actions lack power.

You see, faith is meant to look like something. To be detectable, noticeable, alive. Faith in a forgiving God, should cause us to forgive. Faith in our eternal home, should cause us to breathe when we feel like foreigners in this world. Faith in God's love, should give us relational security. Faith in our Father's adoption of us, should let us know we belong. Outward transformation is inevitable because faith changes us and the way we see the world.

Faith without works is as objectionable as someone saying she has confidence, yet is unwilling to venture outside her home, or someone saying he is content, while screaming in anger. Confidence allows people to interact with the world around them. Contentment staves off bouts of aggression. These abstract concepts are known because they dictate certain behaviors. Likewise, faith is known to exist because it causes people to act in Christ-like ways.

Faith causes couples to overcome even when the odds are stacked against them. It causes people to hope for freedom when they've fallen a hundred times. It causes friends to forgive, parents to reach out one more time, and prayers to be cried out with expectancy. It causes people to give up their own desires so they can feed a hungry child, make friends with a new person at work, and be a neighbor who helps. Faith shows itself through second chances, vulnerability, and selfless love. Faith reveres the Lord to such an extent the answer is, "Yes," to whatever He asks; and faith is intimate to such an extent one can flourish no matter what it requires.

In James 2:17 NIV, James is not teaching faith and works are equal, or suggesting works bring about salvation. He is emphasizing we can't sit around talking about faith, doing bible studies about faith, praying about faith, and therefore say we have faith. Faith is being so convinced God is present, and powerful, we can think of no better option than obeying Him.

Look back again at James 2:14-16.

What is the example James gives to illustrate a lack of faith?

This point is reiterated by John as well.

Write out 1 John 3:17 below.

_____

_____

Both verses pinpoint faith accompanied by action, not a token word with no power to help.

Read James 1:22-25. James urges us to be impacted by what we learn about God. He tells us to let it permeate into our actions. What metaphor does he use to illustrate the senselessness of learning from God, then failing to live differently because of it? (vs 23-24)

_____

_____

Verse 25 NIV states the opposite effect. Fill in the blanks below.

"But whoever looks intently into the perfect law that gives _____ , and continues in it—not forgetting what they have heard, but _____ it—they will be _____ in what they do."

Faith is an incredible gift. It makes obedience a no-brainer. It makes our will less appealing than His. It motivates us to worship Him, rather than be pre-occupied with ourselves. This provides countless opportunities for action. Trusting the truth about God allows us to behave differently than the knee-jerk reaction of our flesh. Faith equips us to move in a manner that flows out of who God is and what He does, rather than who we are and what we want. Faith in action is full of vitality. Faith without action is dead.

Have you struggled to understand the interplay between faith and works? If so, try to put words to your difficulties with these concepts.

_____

_____

_____

_____

_____

_____

_____

_____

Victory

We are created and purposed by God. We are equipped through His authority and power. We are assisted by the intercession of Jesus Christ. All in all, we are positioned for victory. Victory is won in every moment we revere God and experience intimacy with Him in such a manner that our faith thrives.

Read the following verses and record what they teach you about victory below.

1 John 4:4 _____

Isaiah 40:29-31 _____

1 Corinthians 4:20 _____

Psalm 68:35 _____

John 16:33 _____

God is greater than His opposition. He gives power and strength to those who need Him. The Lord is victorious in this world and when we participate with Him through faith in His creation, purpose, and equipping of us, we share in His victory.

I used to think victory would be like a Super Bowl win. I thought it would be a grand, life-changing instant—one that could be marked and counted. Yet, the more I walk with God, the more I realize victory is a thousand little moments where faith wins out and freedom is found.

When we focus on Jesus as the prize we seek, when we trust His guidance most, when we risk our comfort to enjoy a moment's awareness of His presence—this is when we become victorious. I don't mean a glorious, once-for-all victory. I'm referring to a simple string of inconspicuous moments, one by one, where our desire to catch a glimpse of the Lord temporarily overrules everything else. This kind of life is courageous, and free, and it fills us with hope and passion.

Faith in Jesus makes us better than we are. I love the victory He can give in my life and in yours.

In response to God sharing victory with you, express your gratitude to Him. If this is difficult because you have an area where you do not yet know victory, express your longing for it and ask Him for three minutes of freedom. Let your big win form one victorious moment at a time.

_____

_____

_____

_____

_____

_____

_____

_____

_____

_____

_____

Dive Deeper 6

···•●•···

I Praise You, O God

Write out Psalm 146:1-2.

_____

_____

_____

_____

_____

As we come to our last day of study together, I am filled with wonder over our great God. This book has been a journey of faith for me as I hope it has been for you also. I remember a short time ago, thinking it would take a miracle to be writing this last lesson. I have felt anxious, exhilarated, frustrated, full of joy, full of tears, sometimes desperate, and others, confident in Christ. To live by faith is not comfortable, but so worth the risk.

Describe your journey toward big, fresh faith over the last six weeks?

_____

_____

_____

_____

_____

Before we begin our final exploration, let's praise God together.

┌─ *Example* ──────────────────────────────────
│
│    *Oh God, I lift up Your name. I praise You for who You are and for what You do.*
│   *You are majestic and merciful. You are powerful and gracious. You are awesome*
│   *and yet You grant us confidence to approach You. My God, You are worthy of our*
│   *reverence, and You are familiar with us in intimacy. I extol Your name. I applaud*
│   *Your plans. You, my Lord, come through on Your promises. I thank You from the*
│   *depths of my heart.*
│
└──

You can pray along with this sample prayer or write one below to better communicate your thoughts and feelings.

_____

_____

_____

_____

_____

_____

_____

Listen and Confess

Be patient. Sit and wait before God. Listen to what rattles around in your mind and in your heart. Do you sense any conviction of sin, awareness of distraction, or impeding negativity? If so, confess these to God.

_____

_____

_____

_____

_____

_____

_____

Review

With hindrances laid aside, ask God to lead you as you review the material from this week. Please do not skip this part, thinking you've already done the work. Learning to learn from God, to be open to His personal instruction, and to seek His voice are rich and deep blessings. I pray you will not settle for your experience of God to remain indirect, learning only through others. God will mentor you—what a thrill!

Write out the key scripture verse for each lesson this week. Then, highlight the main point you learned day by day. Make your reflections personal.

Day 1: Created

Psalm 139:16

_____

_____

_____

Your Main Learning Point

_____

_____

_____

Day 2: Purposed

Ephesians 2:10

_____

_____

_____

Your Main Learning Point

_____

_____

_____

Day 3: Equipped

2 Thessalonians 1:11

_____

_____

_____

Your Main Learning Point

_____

_____

_____

Day 4: Victorious

James 1:22

_____

_____

_____

Your Main Learning Point

_____

_____

_____

Deeper Review

Summarize the most meaningful point for you from each week. Practice candor as you speak with God about each one. Remember, knowledge about God is all for naught, if not to impact our relationship with Him.

Week 1: Faith Forges Ahead

_____

_____

_____

Prayer

_____

_____

_____

Week 2: The Power to Revere

_____

_____

_____

Prayer

_____

_____

_____

Week 3: Intimate Presence

_____

_____

_____

Prayer

_____

_____

_____

Week 4: Revived

_____

_____

_____

Prayer

_____

_____

_____

Week 5: A Fresh Look at the Age-Old Design

_____

_____

_____

Prayer

_____

_____

_____

Week 6: Step into Abundant Life

_____

_____

_____

Prayer

_____

_____

_____

Reflect on the work God has done.

Try to summarize *Big Fresh Faith* in a paragraph or two. Imagine telling a friend the main points of the book.

_____

_____

_____

_____

_____

_____

_____

_____

_____

_____

How has God brought transformation to you over the past six weeks?

_____

_____

_____

_____

Interact with God

Ask God if there are any further changes He desires as a result of what you've learned.

_____

_____

_____

_____

Converse with God about anything else rumbling in your heart or mind as this study comes to a close.

_____

_____

_____

_____

Praise and thank God for what you've learned to be true about Him.

_____

_____

_____

_____

_____

_____

_____

Read Psalm 146. Where you see the pronoun He, or the words Lord or God, change them to You. Pray through this Psalm speaking to God rather than about Him.

_____

_____

_____

_____

_____

_____

_____

_____

_____

_____

_____

Thanks

Friend, thank you for walking this road with me. Writing to you has inspired my faith and entwined our hearts. I hope you are filled with excitement over the truths you have studied. I hope you are eager to celebrate the greatness of God and His merciful invitation to an intimate relationship with Him. I hope you are more confident than ever in how you've been readied for this life of faith no matter what this world throws at you.

Lord, You are holy. You are great. You are merciful and full of love. You teach us, lead us, and allow us to remain with You. You dwell in us and prepare us for the life of faith You set before us. We couldn't do it without You. We need You every moment. Thank You for using me. Thank You for using this friend of mine. What a privilege God—You give what we don't deserve. Please give us ever more freedom through our faith in You until we are secure in heaven. We glorify You, the one true God, who is Father, Spirit, and Son. I pray in the power and authority of Jesus Christ, amen.

Made in the USA
Columbia, SC
18 September 2019